REVEALED
OBAMA'S LEGACY

WILLIAM KOENIG

REVEALED
OBAMA'S LEGACY

WILLIAM KOENIG

REVEALED
OBAMA'S LEGACY

ISBN 978-0-9717347-7-7

Unless otherwise indicated, scripture taken from the New King James Version®. Copyright © 1982 by Thomas Nelson. Used by permission. All rights reserved.

Jim Fletcher; research assistant
Brent Spurlock and Claudia Koenig; cover design

Printed in the United States of America

Koenig—World Watch Daily
For biblically relevant news go to:
www.watch.org

CONTENTS

Introduction 8

1. Who Influenced and Radicalized Obama?................... 25

2. A Muslim Apologist... 49

3. Israel's Existence in Danger and Middle East Chaos.... 64

4. U.S. Military's Cultural Destruction 94

5. LGBT—He Owns It...107

6. Faith on His Terms...130

7. The Legacy: Will America Ever Recover? 146

8. So Help Me God 167

Appendix 1: 179

Appendix 2: 190

About the author 219

Woe unto them that call evil good, and good evil;

that put darkness for light, and light for darkness;

that put bitter for sweet, and sweet for bitter!

(Isaiah 5:20)

Introduction

*Let no man deceive you with vain words: for because of
these things come the wrath of God upon the children of
disobedience. Be ye not therefore partakers with them.*

(Ephesians 5:6–7)

I was deeply moved by the heartfelt joy and emotion of many black Americans—including the ones I visited with the week prior to Barack Obama's January 20, 2009, inauguration in Washington. They were very excited to be at President Obama's inauguration, to see First Lady Michelle Obama and their darling daughters.

Despite the excitement, never before had pro-gay pastors been given a national platform via prayer at the inauguration, along with a bizarre sermon given at the Washington Cathedral when a female reverend began her message with a story attributed to Cherokee Indian wisdom.

President-Elect Barack Obama asked Gene Robinson, the openly gay Episcopal bishop of New Hampshire, to deliver the invocation at an inaugural event on Sunday, January 18, 2009, on the steps of the Lincoln Memorial.

Gay rights advocates saw the move as a way to compensate for Obama's decision to give Pastor Rick Warren, a prominent pastor from California who opposed same-sex marriage, the high-profile role of delivering the invocation at the inauguration next week.

Furthermore, Obama's invitation to Rick Warren was a way of thanking him for hosting him and former Republican presidential candidate Sen. John McCain at the Saddleback Civil Forum on the Presidency. That nationally televised event greatly helped boost Obama's national exposure.

In preparation for the inauguration event, Bishop Robinson said he had been reading inaugural prayers through history and was "horrified" at how "specifically and aggressively Christian they were."

"I am very clear," he said, "that this will not be a Christian prayer, and I won't be quoting scripture or anything like that. The texts that I hold as sacred are not sacred texts for all Americans, and I want all people to feel that this is their prayer."[1]

Reverend Joseph Lowery gave the inauguration benediction. The following is an excerpt:

> And now, Lord, in the complex arena of human relations, help us to make choices on the side of love, not hate; on the side of inclusion, not exclusion; tolerance, not intolerance.
>
> And as we leave this mountain top, help us to hold on to the spirit of fellowship and the oneness of our family. Let us take that power back to our homes, our

1   Gay Bishop Is Asked to Say Prayer at Inaugural Event
http://www.nytimes.com/2009/01/13/us/13prayer.html?_r=0

workplaces, our churches, our temples, our mosques, or wherever we seek your will.

Lord, in the memory of all the saints who from their labors rest, and in the joy of a new beginning, we ask you to help us work for that day when black will not be asked to get in back, when brown can stick around ... when yellow will be mellow ... when the red man can get ahead, man; and when white will embrace what is right. That all those who do justice and love mercy say "Amen."[2]

In 2009 writing, Dr. Lowery wondered out loud, "How could the church, because of a person's sexual orientation, deny ministry to those whom God has called?" He then suggested that he would prefer to err on the side of inclusion rather than exclusion.[3]

The main sermon for the National Day of Prayer service the day after the inauguration was given by Reverend Sharon E. Watkins, general minister and president of Disciples of Christ Church.[4]

Vote.com wrote that President Obama met Rev. Watkins while on the campaign trail and was deeply moved by how she was able to unite people through prayer.

From the beginning of her sermon, "Harmonies of Liberty":[5]

Mr. President and Mrs. Obama, Mr. Vice President and Dr. Biden, and your families, what an inaugural

---

2   http://voices.washingtonpost.com/inauguration-watch/2009/01/transcript_of_rev_lowerys_inau.html
3   The Rev. Joseph E. Lowery, Former President of SCLC Signs the United Methodists of Color for a Fully Inclusive Church Statement, http://www.umaffirm.org/gcnews10.html
4   General Minister And President Sharon E. Watkins Selected To Deliver Sermon At National Prayer Service, http://disciples.org/ogmp/news-and-updates-from-the-ogmp/general-minister-and-president-sharon-e-watkins-selected-to-deliver-sermon-at-national-prayer-service/
5   Watkins' sermon: Harmonies of Light
http://content.usatoday.com/communities/religion/post/2009/01/61711778/1#.Vx_cm2BX_ww

celebration you have hosted! Train ride, opening concert, service to neighbor, dancing till dawn …

And yesterday … With your inauguration, Mr. President, the flame of America's promise burns just a little brighter for every child of this land!

She used a Cherokee Indian story to explain a person's internal battle rather than the Bible:

One evening a grandfather was teaching his young grandson about the internal battle that each person faces.

"There are two wolves struggling inside each of us," the old man said.

"One wolf is vengefulness, anger, resentment, self-pity, fear …

"The other wolf is compassion, faithfulness, hope, truth, love …"

The grandson sat, thinking, then asked: "Which wolf wins, Grandfather?"

His grandfather replied, "The one you feed."

White House Posting

US Supreme Court Chief Justice Roberts made a mistake in applying the oath to President-Elect Barack Obama. Roberts and Obama redid the oath the next day on January 21 at the White House without a Bible.

The White House posted on its website immediately after the inauguration positions that are totally opposed to the Bible. The new Obama White House boldly and unabashedly added LGBT (lesbians, gays, bisexuals, and transgender) discrimination under civil rights. The posting stated that Obama favored eliminating "don't ask, don't tell" in the US military and much more.

The Extent of Present and Long-Term Damage

It is hard to fully comprehend and extrapolate the extent of present and long-term damage that has and will come from the eight years Barrack Obama has been president of the United States. It will be much worse than God-fearing, Bible-believing Christians could have ever imagined.

President Obama calls himself a Christian, but time and time again he has lectured conservative Christians. His speeches at national prayer events and public events, along with his policies, are a direct affront to the God of the Bible.

In a 2004 interview with Cathleen Falsani, Obama said:

> So, I'm rooted in the Christian tradition. I believe that there are many paths to the same place, and that is a belief that there is a higher power, a belief that we are connected as a people. That there are values that transcend race or culture, that move us forward, and there's an obligation for all of us individually as well as collectively to take responsibility to make those values lived.[6]

In a November 2012 interview, Rick Warren, who praised President Barack Obama's "courage" for inviting him to give the invocation at his 2009 inauguration and hailed his "commitment to model civility," drastically changed his tone on the man who helped make him a familiar name to many Americans.

---

6   Barack Obama and The God Factor Interview
https://sojo.net/articles/transcript-barack-obama-and-god-factor-interview

Obama is "absolutely" unfriendly to religion and his administration's policies have "intentionally infringed upon religious liberties," Warren said in an interview.[7]

When there is public question about Obama's faith, he takes his family to a church with the White House press and photographers in tow, who are quick to tell their readers, "See, Obama is a Christian." That has happened a few times, and these are almost the only times you will see his family in church.

Obama frequently invited to the White House's Easter Prayer breakfasts an assortment of Marxist pastors, lesbian reverends, gay bishops, and pro-LGBT pastors, interspersed with a few conservative pastors and Christian leaders.

Obama remarked in his National Prayer address of February 5, 2015, "And lest we get on our high horse and think this is unique to some other place, remember that during the Crusades and the Inquisition, people committed terrible deeds in the name of Christ. In our home country, slavery and Jim Crow all too often was justified in the name of Christ."[8]

President Barack Obama went off script during remarks at the White House Easter Prayer Breakfast Tuesday, April 7, 2015, to say he is concerned about Christians who are "less than loving" in their expressions.

After sharing quotes from both the apostle Paul and Pope Francis, Obama went on encourage Americans to love our neighbors as ourselves.

"On Easter, I do reflect on the fact that as a Christian, I am supposed to love," the president continued. "And I have to say that sometimes.

7   Rick Warren, Saddleback Pastor: Obama Has "Infringed'" Upon Religious Liberties http://www.huffingtonpost.com/2012/11/28/rick-warren-obama-religious-liberty_n_2206064.html
8   Remarks by the President at National Prayer Breakfast, February 5, 2015, https://www.whitehouse.gov/the-press-office/2015/02/05/remarks-president-national-prayer-breakfast

when I listen to less-than-loving expressions by Christians, I get concerned. But that's a topic for another day."[9]

When Pope Francis was scheduled to visit the White House in September 2015, the White House invited a pro-abortion nun, the first openly gay Episcopal bishop, and at least two openly gay Catholic activists to be among the thousands invited.[10]

Promotion of Islam

No US president or major world leader has done more to promote Islam than Barrack Hussein Obama.

He bowed to the King of Saudi Arabia in April 2009 at a G-20 summit.[11]

He received Saudi Arabia's highest honor, the King Abdul Aziz Order of Merit award, in June 2009 only a few months into office. (President GW Bush received the award in January 2008, his last year in office.)

He gave a speech to the Muslim world on June 4, 2009, from Cairo, Egypt, with Muslim Brotherhood leaders on the front row but not Egyptian President Hosni Mubarak. The speech was filled with distortions and falsehoods while throwing the doors of America open to Muslims.

Harvard Law School professor Alan Dershowitz, a supporter of Barack Obama's election in 2012, offered a stinging criticism of the president's Middle East policy, suggesting it led to the ISIS crisis and broad instability in the region.

---

9   Obama Concerned About "Less Than Loving" Christians at White House Easter Prayer Breakfast:
http://www.christianpost.com/news/obama-concerned-about-less-than-loving-christians-at-white-house-easter-prayer-breakfast-137070
10   For Pope's visit, Obama invites a pro-abort nun10. , gay Episcopal bishop, and LGBT 'Catholic' activists, https://www.lifesitenews.com/news/for-popes-visit-obama-invites-a-pro-abort-nun-gay-episcopal-bishop-and-lgbt
11   Barack Obama criticized for "bowing" to King Abdullah of Saudi Arabia, http://www.telegraph.co.uk/news/worldnews/barackobama/5128171/Barack-Obama-criticised-for-bowing-to-King-Abdullah-of-Saudi-Arabia.html

"It was big mistake to jump on the Arab Spring enthusiastically, without realizing it was soon going to turn into an 'Arab Winter,'" Dershowitz told WND.[12]

Obama spoke at a Baltimore mosque on February 3, 2016, of all the great things Muslims have done for America but no specifics. He also stated:

> Islam has always been part of America. Starting in colonial times, many of the slaves brought here from Africa were Muslim. And even in their bondage, some kept their faith alive. A few even won their freedom and became known to many Americans. And when enshrining the freedom of religion in our Constitution and our Bill of Rights, our Founders meant what they said when they said it applied to all religions.
>
> Back then, Muslims were often called Mahometans. And Thomas Jefferson explained that the Virginia Statute for Religious Freedom he wrote was designed to protect all faiths—and I'm quoting Thomas Jefferson now—"the Jew and the Gentile, the Christian and the Mahometan."[13]

Obama said Jefferson and John Adams had their own copies of the Koran.

Obama neglected to say the reason Jefferson and Adams had a Koran was because they were trying to figure out the Muslim Barbary pirates, who were hijacking US merchant ships.[14]

---

12   Dershowitz: Obama support of Arab Spring "big mistake"
http://www.wnd.com/2014/09/dershowitz-obama-support-of-arab-spring-big-mistake/
13   Remarks by the President at Islamic Society of Baltimore,
https://www.whitehouse.gov/the-press-office/2016/02/03/
remarks-president-islamic-society-baltimore
14   Jefferson Versus the Muslim Pirates: America's first confrontation with the Islamic world
helped forge a new nation's character, http://www.city-journal.org/html/jefferson-versus-muslim-
pirates-13013.html

He has shown no emotion about the plight of Christians in the Middle East but is extremely zealous when talking about his open-door agenda to the Middle Eastern and North African refugees many of them Muslims. He falsely compared their plight to the Christian pilgrims of the *Mayflower* in his Thanksgiving 2015 address.[15]

Promotion of Immorality and Perverse Sexuality

No earthly leader has done more to promote the lesbian, gay, bi-sexual, and transgender (LGBT) agenda in the United States and around the world than Barrack Obama. He has done more to promote immoral-ity and perverse sexuality than any man in history.

Obama's LGBT agenda has divided the church and the family and is leading to the greatest judgment in the history of the country.

The Victory Fund in 2012, which focuses on electing LGBT leaders to public office, noted that the Obama administration had appointed over 250 "openly LGBT professionals to full-time and advisory positions in the executive branch, more than all known LGBT appointments of other presidential administrations combined."

The Presidential Appointments Project, led by the Gay & Lesbian Victory Institute, serves as a talent bank for openly LGBT professionals seeking opportunities to improve our federal government's policies and processes.[16]

Obama stated at a news conference before the annual LGBT event in June 2011 at the White House, "Let me start out by saying that this administration, under my direction has consistently said we cannot dis-criminate as a country against people on the basis of sexual orientation,

---

15   Weekly Address: This Thanksgiving, Recognizing the Greatness of American Generosity, https://www.whitehouse.gov/the-press-office/2015/11/26/
weekly-address-thanksgiving-recognizing-greatness-american-generosity
16   What America's Top LGBT Leaders Think Obama Must Do Next, http://www.huffingtonpost.
com/david-badash/what-americas-top-lgbt-leaders-think-obama-must-do-next_b_2094040.html

and we have done more in the two-and-a-half years I have been in here than the previous forty-three presidents to uphold that principle.

"Whether it's ending 'don't ask don't tell,' making sure that gay and lesbian partners can visit each other in hospitals, making sure that federal benefits can be provided to same-sex couples," he added.[17]

Barack Obama misled Americans for his own political benefit when he claimed in the 2008 election to oppose same sex marriage, his former political strategist David Axelrod wrote in a new book, *Believer: My Forty Years in Politics.*

Axelrod writes that he knew Obama was in favor of same-sex marriages during the first presidential campaign, even as Obama publicly said he only supported civil unions, not full marriages. Axelrod also admits to counseling Obama to conceal that position for political reasons. "Opposition to gay marriage was particularly strong in the black church, and as he ran for higher office, he grudgingly accepted the counsel of more pragmatic folks like me, and modified his position to support civil unions rather than marriage, which he would term a 'sacred union,'" Axelrod writes.[18]

In 2011, the Department of Justice (DOJ) took the position that a central provision of the Defense of Marriage Act (DOMA) was unconstitutional and would no longer defend it in court.

In 2012 Obama became the first sitting president to publicly support same-sex marriage.

In his January 2013 inauguration speech, he stated, "Our journey is not complete until our gay brothers and sisters are treated like anyone

---

17   President Obama Gov Most Pro-Gay in U.S. History,
http://www.christianpost.com/news/obama-my-administration-is-most-pro-gay-in-history-52019/
18   Axelrod: Obama Misled Nation When He Opposed Gay Marriage In 2008, http://time.com/3702584/gay-marriage-axelrod-obama/

else under the law. For if we are truly created equal, then surely the love we commit to one another must be equal as well."[19]

In 2013, the Supreme Court agreed with the administration's position on DOMA and struck down a key part of that law.

In 2014, the president signed an executive order barring employment discrimination against LGBT individuals by federal contractors and subcontractors.

In June of 2015, the United States Supreme Court delivered a momentous victory by recognizing a constitutional right for same-sex couples to marry—making marriage equality the law of the land—a position the president and Justice Department vigorously supported. They joyously celebrated the victory by lighting up the White House in rainbow colors. "With our belief that love means love, there is now no such thing as same sex marriage; just marriage."[20]

On June 26, 2015, the day the Supreme Court voted five to four in favor of same-sex marriage, Obama wrote on Twitter, "Today is a big step in our march toward equality. Gay and lesbian couples now have the right to marry, just like anyone else. #LoveWins."[21]

Evangelical leader Franklin Graham said that President Barack Obama's decision to light up the White House with rainbow colors celebrating the US Supreme Court's ruling on same-sex marriage was a "slap in the face" of "millions of Americans" who did not agree with the decision.

"This is outrageous—a real slap in the face to the millions of Americans who do not support same-sex marriage and whose voice is being

19   Obama presses for gay marriage in inaugural speech,
http://www.usatoday.com/story/news/politics/2013/01/21/
obama-inauguration-speech-gay-marriage-stonewall/1851999/
20   The Supreme Court Rules that Gay and Lesbian Couples Can Marry, https://www.whitehouse.gov/blog/2015/06/26/
live-updates-lovewins-supreme-court-rules-gay-and-lesbian-couples-can-marry-0
21   A Look Back at an Out-Standing Year for LGBT Advocacy,
http://www.huffingtonpost.com/valerie-jarrett/out-100-ally-of-the-year_b_8558950.html

ignored. God is the one who gave the rainbow, and it was associated with His judgment. God sent a flood to wipe out the entire world because mankind had become so wicked and violent. One man, Noah, was found righteous and escaped God's judgment with his family," Graham said on Facebook on Monday, June 29, 2015.

"The rainbow was a sign to Noah that God would not use the flood again to judge the world. But one day God is going to judge sin—all sin. Only those who are found righteous will be able to escape His judgment."[22]

On April 18, 2016, the US Commission on Civil Rights, by a majority vote, strongly condemned recent state laws passed and proposals being considered under the guise of so-called religious liberty, which target members of LGBT community for discrimination.[23]

> The commission approved a report, which will be released shortly, on the issue of religious liberty. In our findings and recommendations the commission makes clear:
>
> - Civil rights protections ensuring nondiscrimination, as embodied in the Constitution, laws, and policies, are of preeminent importance in American jurisprudence.
>
> - Religious exemptions to the protections of civil rights based upon classifications such as race, color, national origin, sex, disability status, sexual orientation, and gender identity, when they are permissible, significantly infringe upon these civil rights.

---

22   Franklin Graham Says LGBT rainbow-colored White House is "slap in the face" of "millions of Americans"; White House calls it "victory"—http://goo.gl/dXMZaL
23   The U.S. Commission on Civil Rights Statement Condemning Recent State Laws and Pending Proposals Targeting the Lesbian, Gay, Bisexual, and Transgender Community, http://www.usccr.gov/press/2016/PR_Statement_LGBTDiscrimination.pdf

- Overly broad religious exemptions unduly burden nondiscrimination laws and policies. Federal and state courts, lawmakers, and policy-makers at every level must tailor religious exceptions to civil liberties and civil rights protections as narrowly as applicable law requires.

Commission Chairman Martin R. Castro stated on behalf of the Commission, "Religious freedom is an important foundation of our nation. However, in the past, 'religious liberty' has been used to block racial integration and anti-discrimination laws. Those past efforts failed and this new attempt to revive an old evasive tactic should be rejected as well. The North Carolina and Mississippi laws, and similar legislation proposed in other states, perverts the meaning of religious liberty and perpetuates homophobia, transphobia, marginalizes the transgender and gay community and has no place in our society."

The target of the secular humanist/ liberals is to make speaking against LGBT and Islam crimes.

The US Constitution's right of free speech is under attack. Christian pastors and believers will be targeted. This is a domestic war of enormous size and consequence birthed during Obama's time in office.

Introduced in December 2015, House Resolution 569 condemns violence, bigotry, and hateful rhetoric toward Muslims in the United States. At press time has received 141 cosponsors, all Democrats.

It was originally referred to House Judiciary committee, who has sent it to Subcommittee on the Constitution and Civil Justice.

Obama's actions caused the Department of Education to demand LGBT compliance of US schools.

His State Department led by Hillary Clinton actively promoted the LGBT agenda on nations and tied it to foreign aid. Some nations rebuked them.

His Labor and Commerce Department actively pushed for nondiscrimination based on sexual orientation with Obama's executive orders.

Military Morale Plummeted

Obama's decisions have decimated the morale of our once-proud military. He has removed generals, reneged on budget promises, and forced the military to get rid of "don't ask, don't tell." His activities and policies have forced Christian chaplains to leave the military.

Former Defense Secretary Robert Gates sharply questioned President Obama's "passion" for military matters in his memoir and claims that practically the only time he saw that in the president was during his push to repeal "don't ask, don't tell."

The former Pentagon chief said in an interview with Fox News that he was "disturbed" by Obama's "absence of passion" when it came to his military strategy. In the book *Duty*, reviewed by Fox News, he wrote, "One quality I missed in Obama was passion, especially when it came to the two wars."[24]

Israel: We Have Your Back

Obama told Israel that the United States had their back in May 2010 but selected people to represent him in the Middle East who were not friends of Israel.[25]

---

24   Gates: "Don't ask, don't tell" fight was only time Obama showed "passion'" for military issues, http://www.foxnews.com/politics/2014/01/12/gates-dont-ask-dont-tell-fight-was-only-time-obama-showed-passion-for-military.html
25   Obama to people of Israel: America has your back, http://nypost.com/2015/05/22/obama-to-people-of-israel-america-has-your-back/

Then out of desperation for a legacy, he and Secretary of State John Kerry led an international effort to forge a nuclear deal with Iran that will greatly endanger Israel, Saudi Arabia, and every Sunni Muslim country that borders the Persian Gulf and every major economy in the world.

Over $100 billion is being released to the number one state sponsor of terrorism in the world. Since the agreement, Iran's leadership continues to call the United States the great Satan and Israel the little Satan.

Claire Lopez, a former CIA agent who is now with the Center for Security Policy, stated recently that Obama has essentially the same goals in the Middle East as the late Osama bin Laden: "to remove American power and influence, including military forces, from Islamic lands."[26]

Deterioration in Every Area of Life

Under Obama, America has experienced the rapid deterioration in every area of life. Most people don't realize the extent of this because 85 to 90 percent of the US media is totally committed to the same things, so they don't report the news or are careful about how they present it.

Obama and his attorney general refused to defend certain marriage and immigration laws that have led to unprecedented lawlessness.

His words and policies have led to the greatest racial division between whites, blacks, and Hispanics in modern history rather than improving them, which so many of his backers and others who voted for him had hoped for.

Millions of illegal aliens have flooded the United States unabated during Obama's terms. Plus he is actively attempting to add many more from the Middle East and Northern Africa that are mostly Muslims.

---

26   Mideast expert: Obama switched sides in war on terror
http://www.wnd.com/2014/08/cia-expert-obama-switchedsides-in-war-on-terror/

No president has overseen such a rapid and sizeable increase in US federal debt, which is projected to pass $20 trillion before Obama leaves office, almost doubling in his eight years in office. The Federal Reserve debt increased over $4.5 trillion due to quantitative easing and lowered interest rates to zero and recently a 0.25 percent. The whole economic boom during his two terms was funded by massive debt, with only a small percentage of Americans benefiting.

Orchestrated Disasters

Is this intentional devastation to America's Judeo-Christian foundation based on the teaching of his mentor Sal Alinsky, the one who dedicated his first printing of the *Rules of Radicals* book to Satan? These actions have not been by accident or coincidental but intentional. Israeli journalist Ruthie Blum wrote, "What the Axis of Evil Owes Obama."[27]

This is not to say that rising from modest means to becoming the head of the United States and by extension, the leader of the free world is not already about as grand as one can get. But it is America's greatness—not Obama's—that enabled him to make it to the White House in the first place.

His ability to pull off winning the election a second time, in spite of a bad economy and the sweeping radicalization of the Middle East, is a measure of how well he had already implemented the methods of his mentor, *Rules for Radicals* author Saul Alinsky, of infiltrating the country's institutions and destroying them from within.

"One thing is clear, however: his presidency has been paved not with failures, but with a string of the most successfully orchestrated disasters in history."[28]

---

27   Israeli journalist Ruthie Blum: What the Axis of Evil Owes Obama, http://www.jpost.com/Opinion/What-the-axis-of-evil-owes-Obama-415420
28   Ibid.

In closing, we have attempted to connect many dots in this book. And that is no easy task with so many life-impacting events happening so frequently.

WHO INFLUENCED AND RADICALIZED OBAMA?

CHAPTER 1

A man's private and public character always move together.[29]

—*Levi Parsons*

H E IS A THOUGHTFUL BOY. SITTING IN PARADISE, on the beach in Honolulu, he squints and gazes at the surf. The sun is shining on his face, and his serene but expressive face takes it all in. His origins, so much the stuff of controversy today, began with a white mother from the Midwest,and a father from Africa. The boy's beginnings were, like all humans, beyond his control, but they took him to exotic places both in body and spirit.

He rises from the beach, hearing his mother's call.

The man who would become Barack Obama remembers all this vividly, writing in his autobiography, *Dreams from My Father*, about the beauty of his first home:

---

29   Eli Mizrachi ,*Two Americans Within the Gates*, (The McDougal Publishsing Company, Hagerstown, MD, 1995), 66.

I can retrace the first steps I took as a child and be stunned by the beauty of the islands. The trembling blue plane of the Pacific. The moss-covered cliffs and the cool rush of Manoa Falls, with its ginger blossoms and high canopies filled with the sound of invisible birds. The North Shore's thunderous waves, crumbling as if in a slow-motion reel. The shadows off Pali's peaks; the sultry, scented air.

Born in the early months of the Kennedy Administration, Barry Soetoro was leaving Hawaii with his mother to join his stepfather in yet another exotic place, this time in Jakarta, Indonesia.

Africa. Kansas. Hawaii. Indonesia. Catholic school. Public school. Homeschool.

And of course, the Muslim education he received in Indonesia adds to this international stew that nourished him in his formative years. For young Barry sometimes accompanied his stepfather, Lolo Soetoro, to a local mosque for Friday prayers.

The biographer Stephen Mansfield has written in *The Faith of Barack Obama* that the forty-fourth president of the United States was raised early on in an environment of atheism, folk Islam, and humanism. This at a time in America when most boys experienced an "Opie Taylor existence."

Obama is, many believe, the most polarizing figure to ever sit in the Oval Office, and that's saying something! And while conservatives can rightly be infuriated by his progressive agenda, it does help to close one's eyes and imagine that boy squinting into the sun setting over the Pacific, as he drank in the "sultry, scented air."

He came from somewhere, and with his background, it was virtually certain that he would end up as a disciple of some of the most radical, leftist figures of the past century. It doesn't excuse some of his decisions, mind you—we'll be dealing with the fallout from his legacy for a very long time—but it does give one a flesh-and-blood picture of the man, rather than the caricature concocted over the course of his two terms as president.

When the Age of Obama dawned on America, like a too-bright light suddenly emerging, the world's lone superpower was sleepwalking through the final days of the George W. Bush presidency—a presidency marked by a protracted fight against a new threat:

Jihad.

Since two planes slammed into the World Trade Center on September 11, 2001, thus shaking our foundations on a deceptively sunny morning, the United States had been fundamentally the same for decades, with older, statesmen-like presidents who were more like managers than ideologues. America still waved flags on the Fourth and enjoyed, if not affection, respect around the globe.

That all changed when the mysterious young man from Illinois(?) outclassed even the meteoric rise of James Earl Carter a generation before.

The official bio is that Obama was born in Hawaii, in 1961, to a Kenyan father and a white mother (from Wichita, Kansas). He graduated from Columbia University and Harvard Law School.

After Obama's biological father died in a car crash, his mother married an Indonesian named Lolo Soetoro, who took the young Obama to Indonesia (near Jakarta), where he lived from ages six to ten.

It was in his later years, as a community organizer and civil rights lawyer in Chicago, that he became acquainted with pro-Palestinian apologists.

Barack Hussein Obama almost literally came out of nowhere to assume the highest office in the world. As president-elect in 2008, he ominously declared that within days, he would fundamentally transform America.

He has, beyond our wildest nightmares.

Americans are, if nothing else, hopeful, forgiving, and willing to give a fellow the benefit of the doubt. Carter, George W. Bush, and even Bill Clinton enjoyed a measure of bipartisan support when they emerged to become president. They looked and sounded the part.

Not so with Obama.

The Illinois legislator, fresh off two years as a US senator, was a puzzle from the beginning for many Americans. One of the things that propelled him to the Oval Office, though, was a gauzy "hope and change" mantra that in its thinness was good enough for scores of first-time voters. Indeed, Obama utilized social media and youth connections like no other candidate before to become president.

The problem was, few knew much of anything about him. And that was a dangerous proposition as we navigated life in a sea of radical Islamist threats.

Who was this guy? How would he fare in a crisis? What did he know about managing a superpower? Most importantly, what did he believe?

It is interesting to note that while the usual suspects gave Obama a pass in terms of scrutiny … so did religious leaders.

In hindsight, the "civil forum" hosted by Pastor Rick Warren at southern California's Saddleback Church, which introduced Barack Obama to mainstream evangelical Christian audiences, was a major boost for the man who aimed to become America's first black president.

In fact, Warren seemed eager to give Obama a helping hand, lobbing softball questions and giving him at least the appearance of endorsement while the hapless John McCain shifted uncomfortably in his chair.

That Obama could win the presidency while also revealing almost nothing of substance about his personal background is a testament both to his cunning and to those helping hands from folks like Rick Warren.

It all calls to mind the searing book by Paul Kengor, *Dupes*, in which the political science professor pulled back the curtain on Soviet attempts to have influence in America, beginning in the '30s. This effort to mainstream Marxist principles into the fabric of our culture has largely proven to be successful, and Obama himself is only the latest evidence.

In his small e-book, *Saul Alinsky: The Evil Genius Behind Obama*, expert researcher and bestselling author Jerome Corsi provides a glimpse into Obama's ideology. It was an ideology developed early on, so that, for example, Obama's marginalizing of Israel in favor of the Palestinian narrative begins to make sense for those who have watched with dismay as he cozies up to radical regimes at the expense of tried-and-true allies.

Corsi writes that Alinsky, the "pioneer of community organizing" (a benign-sounding label if there ever was one), had a profound influence on the young Obama:

> The truth is that Alinsky was a hardline power politics tactitian who cut his teeth in the 1930s by aligning himself with then nationally prominent labor union organizer John L. Lewis, as the two joined forces to unionize workers in Chicago's famed stockyards to demand higher pay. Alinsky's clearly stated goal was revolutionary—to organize poor and minority communities as "power to the people" political force capable of overturning the established order to obtain income redistribution from the "haves" to the "have-nots." That government should force the "haves" to relinquish their

property to the "have-nots" is an idea central to social-ism and communism alike, equally as the idea is at the center of Alinsky and Obama's politics.[30]

Although these links to Obama's Marxist upbringing are not so well known, Newt Gingrich alluded to them during the 2012 Republican presidential primaries.

(It is worth noting that Obama is not the only well-placed politician to endorse Alinsky. While a student at Wellesley College, Hillary Rodham Clinton wrote her thesis on Alinsky.)

As Corsi pointed out in *Alinsky*:

> An honest review of Alinsky's life and his writings makes clear that Barack Obama has lifted his divisive power-politics tactics from Saul Alinsky so completely that the class warfare themes Obama articulates in his speeches running for reelection in 2012 come almost word-for-word from the Saul Alinsky "rules for radicals" playbook.[31]

Alinsky was a native of Chicago, having been born there in 1909, to Russian Jewish immigrants.

Incredibly, in his 1971 book, *Rules for Radicals*, Alinsky dedicated his work to Satan! Read it for yourself (later editions left out this dedication):

> Lest we forget at least an over-the-shoulder acknowledgment to the very first radical: from all our legends, mythology, and history (and who is to know where mythology leaves off and history begins—or which is which), the first radical known to man who

---

30   Jerome R. Corsi, *Saul Alinsky: The Evil Genius Behind Obama* (Paperless Publishing, Kindle Edition, 2012), Kindle locations 31–34.
31   Ibid., 37–39.

rebelled against the establishment and did it so effectively that he at least won his own kingdom—Lucifer.[32]

—Saul Alinsky

Corsi notes the characteristics of Alinsky that his most famous disciple has come to embrace:

> The acknowledgments to the original edition of Alinsky's seminal work, *Rules for Radicals*, leave no doubt that Alinsky considered himself the dark genius of power politics. His goal was 'to stand like a man' in rebelling against the established law and order in the United States which he saw written in favor of the "haves"—the bankers, business owners, management and capitalists—in order to rewrite history in favor of the "have-nots"—the poor, the minorities, the workers and the labor unions.[33]

In terms of practical matters and political ideology, Alinsky's methods dovetailed with what we see today from Obama:

> Barack Obama used Alinsky's vision of "hope and change" to run for president successfully in 2008, and today he is re-crafting Alinsky's admittedly radical and revolutionary consciousness for social justice into the foundational themes of his 2012 presidential campaign. In 2008, Obama's advisors packaged and sold him to American voters as if he were a great unifier. Today, Obama's presidential campaign is pure Alinsky, as Obama campaigns on the theme "The rich should pay their fair share of taxes." Alinsky taught "community organizers" how to focus on grievances, including hatred of those who succeed in a free enterprise system.

32 Saul Alinsky, *Rules for Radicals* (New York: Random House, 1971), 6.
33 Corsi, *Saul Alinsky*, 65–68.

> Now, it appears Obama intends to use Alinsky methods
> to divide the rich from the poor, the young from the old,
> majority whites from minorities, and Latino communi-
> ties from Republican Party politics.[34]

Corsi wrote this ahead of the 2012 presidential election, and one can easily see today how Obama is bringing all this methodology to the fore, in fomenting racial violence and continually harping on the Marxist maxim of redistribution of wealth.

It's there for all to see.

Interestingly, Alinsky disagreed with other revolutionaries (such as Malcom X and William Ayers) on tactics, not ideology. This is particularly instructive as we see how closely this is modeled by, for example, Hamas and Fatah—jihadists birds of a feather that nevertheless are united in their hatred for Israel. Likewise, totalitarian ideologues like Alinsky and Obama might differ on certain tactical methods, but not on the ultimate goal—in this case, taking down America as a superpower.

Corsi also points out a key feature of Obama's agenda: lying.

> Alinsky taught organizers to hide their true inten-
> tions in the words they spoke. Denying the truth or just
> plain lying were both acceptable tactics, as long as the
> cause advanced.[35]

Obama does this on a consistent basis, from assuring citizens they can keep their health plans under Obamacare to pledging undying loyalty to Israel at AIPAC, and in the next phase, withholding arms shipments during times of war (see Hamas, 2014).

Further, the utter failure of policies advocated by the likes of Alinsky and Obama seems lost on a generation that voted Obama into office. Historically, it is proven that Communist governments, when "redistributing wealth," condemn the masses to poverty much worse than before.

---

34   Ibid., 84–87
35   Ibid., 160–62.

This is a feature of Obama's transformational policies that is still to be felt by his voting fans.

Before leaving our discussion of Alinsky, let's take a look at a fascinating, anecdotal insight about the man behind Obama, from a great patriot who has been persecuted by the Obama administration, Dinesh D'Souza:

> As a penniless student at the University of Chicago, Saul Alinsky hit upon a clever way to eat meals without having to pay for them. Alinsky—viewed by many progressives as the father of the social justice movement—described this technique in an interview given to Playboy magazine just before his death in 1972.
>
> In those days customers in the university cafeteria system didn't pay the waitress; rather, they went up to the cashier and paid. Alinsky first went to the cashier and ordered a cup of coffee; at that time it cost a nickel. The cashier would write him a ticket listing that price. Then he would go to another cafeteria and order a full meal. The waitress would give him the check for the meal. Alinsky would then pocket the bill for his meal and submit his nickel ticket to the cashier. By switching checks, he was eating full meals and paying just for his cup of coffee.
>
> This is the kind of scam one can see a clever, impoverished slum kid like Alinsky pulling off. What made Alinsky original is that he shared this knowledge with his fellow students and turned it into an organized scam. Alinsky put up signs on the university bulletin board and invited students to attend a presentation, complete with maps of the cafeteria system. Pretty soon he had a

large horde of students signed up for his scam. "We got the system down to a science, and for six months all of us were eating free."[36]

Hence, we see where the Bernie Sanders–led "free stuff" mantra comes from, as time winds down on the Obama years in the White House. One can see the devious methods Alinsky used to game the system. His most famous disciple has brought this scam to an entire generation.

In 1995, when Obama decided to run for the Illinois legislature, he turned to an old friend and Alinsky disciple, Jean Rudd. The latter expressed surprise that Obama wanted to "leave community organizing" for politics, but Obama assured him that, no, he was simply going to use the skills he had learned to community organize on a grand scale—not merely Southside Chicago.

He had a much bigger vision.

The Age of Destruction: The Man Who Made Obama

If voters are not familiar with Saul Alinsky, then they really don't know Frank Marshall Davis. Only a few astute researchers, like David Horowitz and Paul Kengor, have written much about this writer and "labor activist" who would go on to inform so many things that have made up the worldview of Barack Obama.

Davis, a Kansas native who would coincidentally die in Hawaii, was a radical who really embraced Communism, as he was willing to aggressively advocate for it in the face of backlash from Americans who saw what it could do in the United States.

Davis worked for several papers in Chicago and Atlanta before becoming active in various "red" publications, as he sought to convince

---

36   http://www.dineshdsouza.com/news/wnd-profiteering-off-the-social-justice-scam/

Americans that Russia could be a partner in modeling effective civilization. In other words, he was just another Soviet dupe.

Interestingly, in *Dreams from My Father*, Obama mentions a man who knew his grandfather; the man turned out to be Frank Davis. According to a 2008 article in *The Telegraph*, Davis knew Obama's family well; a friend of both, Dawna Weatherly-Williams, remembers clearly that Obama met Davis in 1970:

> Stan had been promising to bring Barry by because we all had that in common—Frank's kids were half-white, Stan's grandson was half-black and my son was half-black. We all had that in common and we all really enjoyed it. We got a real kick out of reality.[37]

According to *The Telegraph*:

> Maya Soetoro-Ng, Obama's half-sister, told the Associated Press recently that her grandfather had seen Mr. Davis was "a point of connection, a bridge if you will, to the larger African-American experience for my brother."
>
> In his memoir, Mr. Obama recounts how he visited Mr. Davis on several occasions, apparently at junctures when he was grappling with racial issues, to seek his counsel. At one point in 1979 Mr. Davis described university as "an advanced degree in compromise" that was designed to keep blacks in their place.[38]

Davis was also the author of a pornographic book in the 1960s and spoke of his bisexuality and interest in sado-masochism and group sex:

> One chapter concerns the seduction by Mr. Davis and his first wife of a 13-year-old girl called Anne."[39]

---

37   http://www.telegraph.co.uk/news/worldnews/barackobama/2601914/Frank-Marshall-Davis-alleged-Communist-was-early-influence-on-Barack-Obama.html
38   Ibid.
39   Ibid.

According to the *Telegraph* article, Davis's alter ego enjoyed a life of debauchery:

> He stated that "under certain circumstances I am bisexual" and that he was "a voyeur and an exhibitionist" who was "occasionally mildly interested in sado-masochism..."[40]

Keep in mind, this is a man who had access to a young Barry Soetoro. In fact, in a poem titled "Pop," written by Obama in 1981 as an Occidental College student, he describes a strange relationship with the older man; it is an intentionally ambiguous pulling back of the curtain to reveal aspects of their relationship:

> Pop
>
> Sitting in his seat, a seat broad and broken
>
> In, sprinkled with ashes
>
> Pop switches channels, takes another
>
> Shot of Seagrams, neat, and asks
>
> What to do with me, a green young man
>
> Who fails to consider the
>
> Flim and flam of the world, since
>
> Things have been easy for me;
>
> I stare hard at his face, a stare
>
> That deflects off his brow;
>
> I'm sure he's unaware of his
>
> Dark, watery eyes, that
>
> Glance in different directions,
>
> And his slow, unwelcome twitches,

---

40   Ibid.

Fail to pass.

I listen, nod,

Listen, open, till I cling to his pale,

Beige T-shirt, yelling,

Yelling in his ears, that hang

With heavy lobes, but he's still telling

His joke, so I ask why

He's so unhappy, to which he replies...

But I don't care anymore, cause

He took too damn long, and from

Under my seat, I pull out the

Mirror I've been saving; I'm laughing,

Laughing loud, the blood rushing from his face

To mine, as he grows small,

A spot in my brain, something

That may be squeezed out, like a

Watermelon seed between

Two fingers.

Pop takes another shot, neat,

Points out the same amber

Stain on his shorts that I've got on mine, and

Makes me smell his smell, coming

From me; he switches channels, recites an old poem

He wrote before his mother died,

Stands, shouts, and asks

For a hug, as I shrink, my

Arms barely reaching around

His thick, oily neck, and his broad back; 'cause

I see my face, framed within

Pop's black-framed glasses

And know he's laughing too.[41]

Whatever the true nature of their relationship, it's clear that the predatory Davis had enormous influence on young Obama, possibly harming him far more than anyone knows.

Another Mentor Further Radicalizes Obama

Eventually, as he began networking in Chicago, Obama also realized it would be useful to attend a church. The church he chose, Trinity United Church of Christ (the UCC is perhaps the most radically liberal denomination in the United States), was led by none other than the Rev. Jeremiah Wright. It was here that Obama more fully formed his political views, driven in large part by Wright's radicalism when it comes to racial views and in his Liberation Theology embrace of the Palestinians.

Just ahead of a March 30, 2012, "Global March on Jerusalem" (coordinated by Israel haters and pro-Iranian groups), Mark Tapson wrote about the radical who Obama sat under for twenty years:

Black liberation theologist Jeremiah Wright, President Obama's spiritual mentor for nearly twenty years, has expressed his anti-white racism, anti-Americanism, and anti-Semitism on too many occasions to enumerate. He has likened Israel to "a dirty word," and accused it of waging genocide against the Palestinians (if so, it's the most incompetent genocide in history, since the

41   The Poetry of Barack Obama, http://www.nytimes.com/2008/05/18/us/politics/18poems. html?_r=0

Palestinian population is one of the fastest-growing in the world). He and unrepentant terrorist Bill Ayers, another former Obama associate, jointly addressed a crowd of pro-Palestinian protesters in Chicago in 2009. Like Ayers, Wright is so radioactive that even Obama finally distanced himself from the firebrand. Asked if he had spoken to Obama since he had taken office, Wright replied, "Them Jews aren't going to let him talk to me." The White House maintains its silence in response to Wright's endorsement of the march on Israel.[42]

Wright, infamous for his "God-**** America!" harangue, is a race-baiter of the first order, and though Obama found it politically necessary to distance himself from Wright after becoming president, he has never repudiated him. One can see clearly that Wright is yet another brick in the anti-Israel wall that holds Obama in a leftist view of the Arab-Israeli conflict.

Wright's ideology is eerily shared by so many others in Obama's orbit.

In a fascinating interview with Frontpage, Paul Kengor shed light on both Frank Davis and another influence on Obama, one Valerie Jarrett, by referencing his book:

> The book is titled, *The Communist: Frank Marshall Davis, The Untold Story of Barack Obama's Mentor*. Frank Marshall Davis was an African-American born in Kansas in 1905 who eventually moved to Chicago and joined Communist Party USA. Notably, he joined the party after the signing of the Hitler-Stalin Pact, a time when many American communists, particularly Jewish-American communists, left the party. They left because Stalin's

---

42   http://www.frontpagemag.com/fpm/127252
radical-left-unites-iran-march-jerusalem-mark-tapson

signing of the pact facilitated and enabled Hitler's invasion of Poland and start of World War II. Frank Marshall
Davis, however, was undeterred. He joined after the
pact.

Worse, Davis, in Chicago, worked for one of the
most egregious communist fronts in the history of this
country: the American Peace Mobilization. Congress
called the American Peace Mobilization "one of the
most notorious and blatantly communist fronts ever
organized in this country" and "one of the most sedi-
tious organizations which ever operated in the United
States." The group's objective was to stop the United
States from entering the war against Hitler—again,
because Hitler and Stalin were allies. American com-
munists were allows loyal Soviet patriots. They literally
swore allegiance to the USSR and its line.[43]

Shockingly, Obama has talked publicly of the influence Davis had
on him:

In his remarks, Obama never identifies Davis as a
communist or even a leftist. But the remarks do reflect
the significant influence that Davis had over his young
life as he was growing up in Hawaii. Obama talks about
how Davis 'schools' him on the subject of race relations.
The term implies a teacher-student relationship the two
of them had, confirming what we had reported back in
2008, that Davis had functioned as Obama's "mentor."

It's important to understand what Obama is
saying here. Getting ready to read directly from his
book, Dreams from My Father, Obama talks about the

---

43   http://www.frontpagemag.com/fpm/221855/
valerie-jarretts-influence-obama-jamie-glazov

> passages ending with "me having a conversation with a close friend of my maternal grandfather, a close friend of gramps, a black man from Kansas, named Frank, actually at the time a fairly well-known poet named Frank Marshall Davis, who had moved to Hawaii and lived there, and so I have a discussion with him about the kinds of frustrations I'm having, and he sorts of schools me that I should get used to these frustrations …"[44]

Even more shocking, evidence may exist that Davis had much more influence on Obama than anyone had previously realized.

Joel Gilbert, who interviewed Obama's brother, Malik, in 2015, unearthed this gem from the brother:

> According to Malik, "There's a great resemblance. I think Frank Marshall Davis and Barack, they look alike. Some kind of moles I see on his face and Frank, he has those too. There's a resemblance."[45]

Now enter the connection to Valerie Jarrett, currently Obama's influential advisor. Kengor says that Jarrett's grandfather, Robert Taylor, was involved in a group called the American Peace Mobilization, another bland-sounding group that really fronted for Communist agendas in the West.

> Valerie Jarrett has additional family roots in these things. Both Taylor (Jarrett's grandfather) and Frank Marshall Davis…would have often encountered another politically active Chicagoan, Vernon Jarrett. In fact, Vernon Jarrett and Frank Marshall Davis worked together on the very small publicity team (a handful

---

44   http://www.aim.org/aim-column/
obama-admits-communist-schooled-him-on-white-racism/
45   http://freedomoutpost.com/bombshell-interview-malik-obama-says-barack-is-dishonest-a-schemer-frank-marshall-davis-may-be-his-real-father/

of people) of the communist-controlled Packinghouse Workers Union.

Who was Vernon Jarrett? He would one day become Valerie Jarrett's father-in-law.

So, to sum up, Obama's mentor, Frank Marshall Davis, worked with the literal relatives of Valerie Jarrett—her grandfather and future father-in-law—in Chicago's Communist Party circles in the 1940s.[46]

Kengor goes further in his uncovering of Obama's true roots:

As readers of this site are aware, I've just published a book on Barack Obama's mentor, Frank Marshall Davis. No president in the long history of this republic has had a mentor like Obama's. Frank Marshall Davis was a literal—and I mean literal—card-carrying member of Communist Party USA. I publish Davis's Communist Party number (47544) on the cover of the book, and fill an appendix with declassified FBI documents and Soviet archival material.

Those documents reveal a Davis so suspicious that he was placed on the federal government's Security Index, which meant he could be immediately arrested if war broke out between the United States and USSR. With that sort of pro-Soviet influence throughout his adolescence (1970-79), Barack Obama would have trouble getting a security clearance for an entry-level government job, let alone sit in the Oval Office.

Nonetheless, Obama sits in that Oval Office today thanks to four factors: the American voter, a scandalously biased media, a skillful election strategy charted

---

46   Ibid.

by David Axelrod, and the careful nurturing of Valerie Jarrett.[47]

Jarrett, of course, today is perhaps the top advisor to both Barack and Michelle Obama. She has been deeply involved in all sorts of nefarious dealings, including the infamous Iranian deal.

A report from *Judicial Watch* pulls back the door on Jarrett's own radical background:

> Valerie Jarrett's late father—a physician named James Bowman—had a lengthy FBI file showing that he was a Communist who often collaborated with other Communists based principally in Chicago. In 1950, for instance, Bowman communicated with a paid Soviet agent named Alfred Stern, who later fled the U.S. to Prague when he was indicted on espionage charges that were ultimately confirmed beyond doubt—specifically, he had conspired to transmit military and political information to the Soviet Union.
>
> Bowman was also a member of the Association of Internes and Medical Students, a group that, according to his FBI file, engaged in un-American activities and "has long been a faithful follower of the Communist Party line."
>
> Valerie Jarrett's mother is the early-childhood-education author Barbara Taylor Bowman (born 1928), who in 1966 co-founded a Chicago-based graduate school in child development known as the Erikson Institute, named after the psychoanalyst Erik Erikson.
>
> In 1950 Erikson became a hero to the Left by choosing to resign from his professorship at the University of

---

47   http://israelmybeloved.com/valerie-jarrett-and-the-president/

California rather than sign an anti-Communist loyalty oath as the school required.

The Erikson Institute's radical orientation is reflected in the fact that its board of trustees has included such figures as Bernardine Dohrn, wife of the former Weather Underground terrorist and lifelong Marxist Bill Ayers, and Tom Ayers, father of the same lifelong Marxist.

Jarrett's maternal grandfather was a Chicagoan named Robert Taylor, the first African-American head of the Chicago Housing Authority. In the 1940s he was involved with such Communist fronts as the American Peace Mobilization and the Chicago Civil Liberties Committee. A fellow member of these groups was Frank Marshall Davis, the Communist journalist who in the 1970s would mentor a young Barack Obama.

An FBI document shows that Taylor, like Valerie Jarrett's father, was believed to have been "in contact" with the aforementioned Soviet agent Alfred Stern "on a number of occasions."

Valerie Jarrett's maternal grandmother, Dorothy Taylor, was an activist with Planned Parenthood in its early years. Planned Parenthood was founded in 1942 by Margaret Sanger, a member of the New York Socialist Party and a eugenicist who favored the use of use birth control to limit the reproduction of society's "least intelligent and fit" members."[48]

---

48   http://www.judicialwatch.org/blog/2015/06/communism-in-jarretts-family/

Jarrett and the Obamas: Beginnings

Valerie Jarrett has factored into the lives of Barack and Michelle Obama for years:

> In media and Washington circles portray Jarrett, who held top positions in Chicago government and business, as a brilliant strategist and thinker who practically runs both wings of the White House and who did as much or more than anyone to put the Obamas there.

> In 1991, Jarrett, then Mayor Rich Daley's deputy chief of staff, offered Michelle Robinson a job in City Hall. Before Michelle accepted, she insisted that Jarrett meet with Michelle's fiancé Barack Obama. Jarrett promptly took both under her wing and, over the years, introduced Barack to the inner Daley circle, to wealthy business people, and to the people who mattered in her enclave, Hyde Park—all of which helped Obama as he moved up from community organizer to Springfield to Washington.

> The reality is that her power stems from friendship with the first couple, forged by after-hour access, total trust that her only motive is to protect the first couple's images and advance their interests. Valerie Jarrett is not powerful because she creates and implements policy, but because she's the last person the president and/or first lady talk to, sometimes over dinner in their private dining room. It was reportedly the Obamas who persuaded Jarrett not to pursue appointment to the President-Elect's vacated U.S. senate seat, but instead to keep close to them in the White House.[49]

---

49   http://www.chicagomag.com/Chicago-Magazine/Felsenthal-Files/January-2014/
The-Mysteries-and-Realities-of-Valerie-Jarrett-Mystery-Woman-of-the-White-House/

If people think Dick Cheney commanded attention in the White House, they should examine Jarrett's hold over the Obamas.

She has unparalleled access:

> At every turning point in Obama's career, Jarrett was there to introduce, to solve or resolve, to console or confirm. She was in the room when Obama decided to run for president. And she was there on a warm summer night in July 2007 when Obama was afraid he was losing to Hillary Clinton.

> Jarrett's White House role is unprecedented. She meets privately with the president at least twice a day with no one else present. Her influence is enormous and wide-ranging. She wields informal power, like a first lady; scheduling power, like a chief of staff; and power over policy, like a special envoy. She has the unusual freedom to put herself in any meeting she chooses and to set the priorities as she sees fit. When *The New York Times's* Robert Draper asked Obama if he "runs every decision past her," the president answered immediately: "Yep. Absolutely."[50]

No Decisions without Jarrett's Input

She is directly involved with every major pivotal decision—Obamacare, LGBT, same-sex marriage, don't ask, don't tell, birth control contraceptives abortion, Iran, etc.

Valerie Jarrett is considered the most powerful woman in Washington. She has guided the president's decisions on health care, the budget, the stimulus, the deficit, and foreign affairs. Among the items bearing her fingerprints:

---

50   http://israelmybeloved.com/valerie-jarrett-and-the-president/

- Jarrett aggressively pushed ObamaCare's passage in Congress.

- Jarrett pushed Obama to take on the Catholic Church over contraception, arguing that it would appeal to single women (she was right) and that religious freedom isn't important (she was wrong).

- White House visitor logs show dozens of visits by top abortion activists.

- Planned Parenthood's president, Cecile Richards, visited the White House numerous times to visit Jarrett

- Cecile Richards met with Michele Obama, Valerie Jarrett, and Nancy Keenan, another abortion leader, at a Women's Leadership Forum in May 2011.

- Ilyse Hogue, president of NARAL, the largest abortion lobby group in the United States, visited the White House several times. Obama and Valerie Jarrett are among the visitors listed at the time of she logged in at the White House.

- Jarrett hailed Obama efforts to end gay "conversion therapy."[5]

- Jarrett said protecting LGBT workers means protecting all workers.[6]

- Valerie Jarrett organized White House rainbow lights to celebrate Supreme Court legalized same-sex marriage.[7]

- Valerie Jarrett was selected by Obama to lead his White House Council on Women and Girls.

- Lt. General Jerry Boykin (ret.) said Rice and Jarrett are calling the shots on ISIS, Iran deal.[8]

Perhaps you are a conservative who has never understood why Obama does the things he does. Or perhaps you are a centrist or independent voter who is also puzzling about the seemingly odd paths Obama takes politically.

Can you see now the connections? The background?

While many of us not only do not like his decisions (in fact, we abhor them), at least now it is easier to *understand* just who Barack Obama is. Like all of us, he came from somewhere. And the people he met on his particular path have affected all of us.

A MUSLIM APOLOGIST

And he will be a wild man; his hand will be against every man, and every man's hand against him; and he shall dwell in the presence of all his brethren.

(Genesis 16:12)

THE SCENE WAS SURREAL.

An American president, a handful of years removed from the horror of 9/11, speaking before a Cairo audience that included the leadership of the Muslim Brotherhood.

Barack Obama was in the mood to apologize and appease.

His own trajectory in thinking after 9/11 fell in line with those who believed "Islamophobia" was getting out of hand.

Obama intended to deliver a watershed speech in Cairo, holding out not only an olive branch, but perhaps an entire olive grove, in order to placate our enemies and those he saw as "moderates." Before stepping foot in Egypt, Obama bowed before the Saudi king, a deferential moment not lost on those who understand the tribal customs of the desert kingdoms.

As he stood in the glare of lights in Cairo on June 4, 2009, Obama looked out to see the who's who of Muslim Brotherhood leadership and ... no sign of Egyptian President Hosni Mubarak. The latter was in the process of drastically underestimating this mysterious new American.

> "*Assalaamu alaykum* [peace be with you]," he said, extending an Arabic greeting only used when one Muslim is addressing another (which the audience necessarily perceived as Obama's way of saying he himself was one of them). "We meet at a time of tension between the United States and Muslims around the world ... fed by colonialism that denied rights and opportunities to many Muslims, and a Cold War in which Muslim-majority countries were too often treated as proxies without regard to their own aspirations. Moreover, the sweeping change brought by modernity and globalization led many Muslims to view the West as hostile to the traditions of Islam.

> "Violent extremists have exploited these tensions in a small but potent minority of Muslims. The attacks of September 11, 2001 and the continued efforts of these extremists to engage in violence against civilians has led some in my country to view Islam as inevitably hostile not only to America and Western countries, but also to human rights ..."[51]

Ruthie Blum's excellent book, *To Hell in a Handbasket: Carter, Obama, and the "Arab Spring,"* details this momentous speech, in which Obama

---

51   Ruthie Blum, *To Hell in a Handbasket: Carter, Obama, and the "Arab Spring,"* Kindle edition (New York: RVP Publishers, 2012), Kindle locations 2097–99.

stroked the egos of the most radical Muslim leadership. (The Muslim Brotherhood's ideology springs directly from the Colonial period, in which the Wahhabi sect in Arabia resurrected the most violent models for advancing Islam in order to establish a new caliphate.)

Blum revealed the underlying message that Obama was sending the Brotherhood:

> To show that he was not merely an American Christian, but rather someone who understood the Muslim mindset and was heartened by it, he recounted, "... As a boy, I spent several years in Indonesia and heard the call of the *azaan* at the break of dawn and the fall of dusk. As a young man, I worked in Chicago communities where many found dignity and peace in their Muslim faith. As a student of history, I also know civilization's debt to Islam..." After waxing poetic about Islam's having been responsible for much of the world's mathematical, architectural and other innovations of cultural and scientific significance, he went on to laud its humanitarianism.

> "... Islam has demonstrated through words and deeds the possibilities of religious tolerance and racial equality," he said, adding that it "has always been a part of America's story... Since our founding, American Muslims have enriched the United States. And I consider it part of my responsibility as President of the United States to fight against negative stereotypes of Islam wherever they appear."

> The stunned and exuberant Muslim Brotherhood-heavy audience couldn't believe their ears. To have such a champion in the Oval Office—one whose stated

objective was to look out for their interests the world over—was more than they had bargained for when they prayed to Allah for him to be elected.[52]

He offered positive rhetoric to appeal to young and moderate Muslims; but reading between the lines, it's clear he has opened the border of America to Islam, and in his speech, he further legitimized Islam and the Koran to the world.

Indeed, the path from Obama's childhood to Cairo was made smoother by another seemingly pacifist American president, James Earl Carter. In fact, the Iranian Revolution, the global terror disaster birthed on Carter's watch, occurred as Obama was coming of age. One wonders what he thought as American embassy staffers were herded, blindfolded, into a yearlong captivity.

No less than Israel's former ambassador to the United States, Michael Oren, openly speculated after the publication of his book, *Ally*, just what would motivate Obama to bend over backward in his attempts to accommodate the Muslim world:

> In the third of a series of stinging op-eds about US President Barack Obama and his relationship with Israel, former Israeli ambassador to the US and current Kulanu MK Michael Oren speculated that the president's persistent outreach to the Muslim world is based on abandonment issues by two Muslim father figures.

> In an article published in Foreign Policy Magazine, Oren asserts that Obama seeks acceptance by the Muslim world to fill a void caused by his abandonment as a younger child. He calls the president's policies and overall view towards the Middle East as naïve.

---

52   Ibid., 2111–14.

"Obama's attitudes toward Islam clearly stem from his personal interactions with Muslims. These were described in depth in his candid memoir, *Dreams from My Father*, published 13 years before his election as president. Obama wrote passionately of the Kenyan villages where, after many years of dislocation, he felt most at home and of his childhood experiences in Indonesia," Oren explained.

I could imagine how a child raised by a Christian mother might see himself as a natural bridge between her two Muslim husbands. I could also speculate how that child's abandonment by those men could lead him, many years later, to seek acceptance by their co-religionists.[53]

Further in the foreign policy piece, Oren considers just why Obama could appear so indifferent (calloused?) in the wake of jihadist attacks on innocents:

"The president could not participate in a protest against Muslim radicals whose motivations he sees as a distortion, rather than a radical interpretation, of Islam," Oren writes about the president's refusal to attend a Paris rally following the terror attacks at the Charlie Hebdo headquarters and a kosher supermarket in Paris.

"If there are no terrorists spurred by Islam, there can be no purposely selected Jewish shop or intended Jewish victims, only a deli and randomly present folks," Oren writes.[54]

Writing in *The Atlantic* ahead of the Cairo speech, Marc Ambinder stated:

53   Lea Speyer, *Breaking Israel News*, June 22, 2015.
54   Ibid.

A sign that the Obama administration is willing to publicly challenge Egypt's commitment to parliamentary democracy: various Middle Eastern news sources report that the administration insisted that at least 10 members of the Muslim Brotherhood, the country's chief opposition party, be allowed to attend his speech in Cairo on Thursday.

The brotherhood is a Salafist/ Islamist party with branches in many countries, and it does not have a reputation for liberalism and has supported violent campaigns against Israel (and Egypt's own government). It has deep roots in the region and traces its intellectual lineage to Sayyid Qutb, a top American-educated Islamic intellectual who was executed—or martyred—by the Egyptian government in 1966. The Brotherhood has direct links with Sunni groups like Hamas in the Palestinian territories. Its standing in Egypt has suffered as of late because of a crackdown by the Egyptian government and a growing frustration that it is too conservative (anti-women's rights, the whole gamut) for a modern Middle East.[55]

Pacifying Jihadists, Collapsing America

Never before have we had a president who is more divisive or a greater threat to our nation's foundation and continued survival than Barack Obama.

His Muslim outreach, which began the day he took office, and his distortion of the truth about Islam have created a lot of confusion and falsehoods. The damage is extensive.

---

55   http://www.theatlantic.com/politics/
archive/2009/06/-brotherhood-invited-to-obama-speech-by-us/18693/

After 9/11, President George W. Bush called Islam a "religion of peace" in order to keep Americans from attacking Muslims. He and members of his administration repeated it many times. President Obama uses the term frequently, and it is false.

The horrific and violent acts of the Islamic State (IS), led by Abu Bakr al-Baghdadi, are what Mohammed would do if he were alive today. This is why a lot of Muslims refuse to speak out against IS.

Claire Lopez, a former CIA officer who is now with the Center for Security Policy, stated recently that Obama has essentially the same goals in the Middle East as the late Osama bin Laden: "To remove American power and influence, including military forces, from Islamic lands."

The damage and confusion in the United States and in the Middle East will have major significance in the days ahead.

In a speech at Fairview Baptist Church in Edmond, Oklahoma in 2012, Frank Gaffney of the Center for Security Policy displayed a stunning graphic that outlines in black and white just how far Obama has gone to mainstream the Muslim Brotherhood:

"Policy Alignment with the Brotherhood's Agenda"

2009: President Obama apologizes for US policy in "Muslim outreach" speech in Cairo, insists Brotherhood representatives be in the audience.

2010: Obama administration officials begin formally "engaging" with Brotherhood officials.

2011: President Obama calls for resignation of Hosni Mubarak.

2011: DNI [Director of National Intelligence] Clapper describes Brotherhood as "largely secular."

2011: United States trains Muslim Brotherhood operatives about how to win elections.

2011: Obama demands Israel return to "1967 borders."

2012: United States transfers $1.5 billion to Egyptian government.

2012: Morsi wins in Egypt—announces he will seek to impose shariah.

2012: United States announces sale of fighters, tanks to Egypt.

2013: Secretary of State Kerry gives Egypt $250 million more.

When we see it that way, it's hard not to come to the conclusion that Barack Obama is more than just an appeaser when it comes to Islam. And while Obama is clearly the most "forward-thinking" American president regarding Islam, there have been serious missteps before him. Witness the time renowned scholar Bernard Lewis was put in a delicate position by the Clinton White House:

> Indeed, it is very hard to cite the Koran, even selectively, for evidence that Islam, like Judaism and Christianity, yearns for peace. In the run-up to the Yitzhak Rabin-Yasser Arafat handshake on the White House lawn in 1993, President Clinton's speechwriters called on the great American scholar of Islam, Bernard Lewis, for a quotation from the Koran that the president could use for the occasion. Lewis cited one from memory. "Not that one," he was told. "We've already used that one. We need another one." Lewis was forced to reply, "I don't think there is another one."[56]

When Oil Became King

In fact, it appears that American political leaders' missteps with Islam (after a promising start with Thomas Jefferson sending the Marines

---

56   Michael A. Ledeen, *Obama's Betrayal of Israel* (New York: Encounter, 2009), 18–19.

to engage Muslim pirates off the coast of Africa) began when the first patch of black gold was found in the Arabian Desert. None other than the historian Michael Oren recounts this breakthrough:

> Eager to break the European monopoly over Middle Eastern oil, the U.S. government for the first time became actively involved in the oil business. In 1921, Secretary of Commerce Herbert Hoover, a seasoned manager of international relief efforts, rallied the seven leading American petroleum companies—New Jersey (later Esso/Exxon), Texas (later Texaco), Sinclair, Mexican, Atlantic, Gulf, and New York (SOCONY, later Mobil)— into a potent consortium. Assailed by this united front, the European companies relented and invited the Americans to join them in forming a new cartel, the Iraq Petroleum Company (IPC). In return for forfeiting their right to explore for oil outside of the IPC framework (the so-called self-denial clause), the Americans received 23.75 percent of all the petroleum extracted from the Middle East. The formula, which satisfied the escalating energy needs of the United States without saddling it with political responsibilities in the Middle East, marked a victory for American diplomacy and a potential bonanza for American oil. The vastness of the riches hidden beneath Iraqi sands was partially revealed in October 1927, when prospectors in the northern city of Kirkurk unleashed a geyser so powerful it killed two of them.[57]

---

57 Michael B. Oren, *Power, Faith, and Fantasy: America in the Middle East: 1776 to the Present*, Kindle Edition. (New York: Norton, 2011), 410–11.

Thus began the pragmatic reason for cozying up to the Arab sheiks. Barely a generation later, oil from the Middle East also proved pivotal in defeating the Nazi advances across North Africa. One can hardly condemn American leaders for seizing upon this prized fossil fuel.

All American presidents, from Coolidge to the Bushes, cultivated at the very least economic relationships with the Saudis, and this in part explains the famous "Arabist" branch of the US State Department. It is important to note that the one "break" in relations, the oil embargo of 1973, occurred not so much because of ideological reasons but pragmatism: Richard Nixon would not let Israel be defeated in the Yom Kippur War. He well knew the Arab nations could not be trusted, and an Israel-free Middle East would be intolerable for America.

Even Jimmy Carter's animus toward Israel had somewhat of a narrow focus—a cessation of hostilities between Israel and the Palestinians—but no American president had developed an affinity for Muslims.

Until 2009.

Barack Hussein Obama, especially in his second term, barely conceals his affinity with Islam. This, coupled with his fang-baring stance toward Israel, causes those in Washington's corridors of power many sleepless nights. As this book was being written, a profoundly dangerous "deal" was being crafted with the Iranians, who are laughing all the way to the bank as they deal with Obama and his chief negotiator, the hapless Secretary of State John Kerry.

Obama's Muslim Connections in the White House

The average person, when I engage them in conversation about these issues, is usually stunned to learn just how deeply jihadists have penetrated the Oval Office. When you understand how closely the Muslim Brotherhood (primarily through the lobby arm, CAIR) advises the president and *his* advisors, the more chilling it all becomes.

Robert Spencer of Jihad Watch is one of the most informed researchers, and his 2013 article in the courageous publication Frontpagemag pulls the curtain back on this diabolical association:

> Obama's support for the Brotherhood goes back to the beginning of his presidency. He even invited Ingrid Mattson, then-president of the Islamic Society of North America (ISNA), to offer a prayer at the National Cathedral on his first Inauguration Day—despite the fact that ISNA has admitted its ties to the Brotherhood. The previous summer, federal prosecutors rejected a request from ISNA to remove its unindicted co-conspirator status. Obama didn't ask Mattson to explain ISNA's links to the Muslim Brotherhood and Hamas. On the contrary: he sent his Senior Adviser Valerie Jarrett to be the keynote speaker at ISNA's national convention in 2009.[58]

There is no lack of evidence of the cozy relationship between the Brotherhood and the Obama White House:

> A Muslim Brotherhood member who recently was hosted at the State Department along with several of the Islamist group's key allies now claims that a White House official also was present in that meeting, according to recent remarks.
>
> Abdel Mawgoud al-Dardery, a Brotherhood member and former Egyptian parliamentarian, was in the United States along with a delegation of fellow Brotherhood leaders and allies.
>
> The Brotherhood-aligned delegation caused an international stir after the Washington Free Beacon

58   http://www.frontpagemag.com/2013/robert-spencer/the-muslim-brotherhoods-man-in-the-white-house/

revealed that it had been hosted for a meeting with several State Department officials.

Another member of the group, a Brotherhood-aligned judge in Egypt, posed for a picture while at Foggy Bottom in which he held up the Islamic group's notorious four-finger Rabia symbol.[59]

And, if possible, the connections become even more sinister. A group called Interfaith Youth Core is headed by a fellow named Eboo Patel, who serves as IFYC's founder and president. He is also a member of President Obama's Advisory Council on Faith-Based Neighborhood Partnerships. (Sound familiar? "Community Organizing," anyone?)

Note the biographical information on Patel, from the IFYC website:

Eboo's core belief is that religion is a bridge of cooperation rather than a barrier of division. He's inspired to build this bridge by his faith as a Muslim, his Indian heritage, and his American citizenship. He has spoken about this vision at places like the TED conference, the Clinton Global Initiative, and the Nobel Peace Prize Forum, as well as college and university campuses across the country. He has written two books about interfaith cooperation, Acts of Faith and Sacred Ground. Some people ask if Eboo ever stops talking about interfaith. If it's any indication, his five-year-old son can define interfaith cooperation.[60]

In a 2009 piece on Patel by U.S. News & World Report writer Bill George let it slip:

In the past year, Patel, 33, has become a leading voice for embracing religious pluralism. He writes "The

59   http://freebeacon.com/national-security/
muslim-brotherhood-white-house-official-met-us-at-state-department/
60   http://www.ifyc.org/about-us/eboo-patel

Faith Divide," a featured column for the *Washington Post*. In February, Obama appointed him to the White House Office of Faith-Based and Neighborhood Partnerships, giving him the platform to push the president to discuss interfaith issues more prominently (as he gently chides Obama for not acknowledging his Muslim heritage). The president appears to be listening. In his Cairo speech in June, Obama addressed the common principles of America and Islam: "justice and progress; tolerance and the dignity of all human beings."[61]

Did you catch that? Patel "gently chides Obama for not acknowledging his Muslim heritage." Thus, we see a peek behind the curtain of what practicing, committed jihadists believe about Obama's true background.

A further chilling plot point involving Eboo Patel is his chummy embrace of ... are you ready for it ... evangelical Christian leaders in America!

None other than Ed Stetzer, president of LifeWay Research, part of the gigantic publishing arm of the Southern Baptist Convention, counts Patel among his friends.

[In 2013] LifeWay Research Division President Ed Stetzer interviewed [Pastor Bob] Roberts about interfaith dialogue with Muslims. Stetzer referenced Eboo Patel as an example of a moderate Muslim, yet Patel—appointed in February 2009 to President Barack Obama's Advisory Council on Faith-Based Neighborhood Partnerships—has a history with the family of Hassan al-Banna, the radical who founded the Muslim Brotherhood in Egypt in 1928. The Brotherhood is the

61   http://www.usnews.com/news/best-leaders/articles/2009/10/22/eboo-patel-obama-faith-adviser-preaches-religious-tolerance

spiritual forefather of today's most lethal terror groups, including Hamas and Al-Qaida.[62]

Stetzer, at his own Christianity Today-run blog, shows that his left-ward leanings are easily documented, as he helped mainstream Eboo Patel for evangelical audiences:

> Eboo Patel, one of the more important thinkers among younger Muslims, writes in Sojourners about how we view Muslims. In the article he mentions an important principle called the "availability heuristic" which basically means we form our perception of a group by those we most often we see from that group. His point is well taken by using the example of African American, he reminds us about the vast majority of Muslims. It's worth your time.[63]

The point Stetzer, Patel, Sojourners, and Christianity Today want to make is that Muslims are unfairly judged based on events like 9/11. The classic (flawed) argument is made that only a tiny number of the planet's billion Muslims are committed jihadists. As has been pointed out by any number of researchers, even if that is true—the numbers are "small"—we are still talking about tens of millions of sleeper cells in the form of Muslim true believers, each wishing to bring down the West.

The question is, why are evangelical leaders like Stetzer doing this?

It is deeply disturbing that Ed Stetzer takes at face value the claims of Eboo Patel that he is a pacifist bridge-builder. As researchers like Frank Gaffney Jr. can attest, nothing could be further from the truth.

Additionally, by paying attention to the writings, speeches, and social media pages of evangelical leaders like Stetzer, we see that they are not only dupes of the Muslim Brotherhood, but they also curry favor

---

62   http://www.jpost.com/Blogs/Christian-World/Evangelicalisms-useful-idiots-363708
63   http://www.christianitytoday.com/edstetzer/2013/march/morning-roundup-030413-what-we-know-about-muslims.html

with Washington political insiders and influencers, including the president himself.

This is a profoundly sad state of affairs and is but one visible marker that America has been infiltrated by an enemy whose malevolence has not been seen since 1933–1945.

ISRAEL'S EXISTENCE IN DANGER AND MIDDLE EAST CHAOS

CHAPTER 3

There are five great items of evidence that are existing today and which nobody can deny or fail to recognize which support the trustworthiness of the Bible. The first is the Jews.[64]

—Robert Dick Wilson

I N THE ANXIOUS MOMENTS AND DAYS THAT FELL in the shadow of the death of Franklin Delano Roosevelt—on vacation at his Warm Springs, Georgia, retreat—the West's political and military leadership breathed a sigh of relief that the twilight of the Axis Powers had come … at the same time a hapless politician from Missouri took the driver's seat in the Oval Office.

Harry S. Truman didn't have the education, social background, breeding, or apparent leadership qualities to maneuver America

---

64   Robert Dick Wilson, *The Princeton Theological Review*, "The Rule of Faith and Life," 430, July 1928.

through a new time of challenge as the Soviet Union took advantage of a war-weary Europe to gobble up territory for its evil empire.

Truman was so much dull dishwater in the wake of the charismatic Roosevelt's sudden death, barely a few months into his fourth term. The iconic decisions about Japan were still months away.

And then something amazing happened. Harry Truman emerged as a fearless, visionary leader. His successful prosecution of the last months of the war tagged him at least as a man who would not roll over.

He would need all that grit, for a truly epic decision lay before him only three years after the war ended.

In late 1947, yet another epic decision lay before Truman.

Palestine.

As the Zionist leaders in the region and in Europe understood, it was now or never after UN Resolution 181 paved the way for a Jewish (and Palestinian Arab) state in historical Palestine. Jewish influencers began to jockey for meetings with Truman and his advisors, but they were rebuffed initially, for various reasons.

David Ben Gurion knew that his team must seize the day as the countdown for Britain's pullout of Palestine began. The empire set a date of May 15, 1948, to leave the area to the battling Jews and Arabs.

As the burgeoning Jewish state needed the backing of a certain superpower, Truman found himself a popular man.

He also found himself on the cusp of a pivotal moment in history, when his background would prepare him for the task at hand.

> Truman's thinking on the Middle East was colored by his Baptist upbringing. Thoroughly versed in Scripture and its depictions of sacred landscapes, Truman, much like American presidents of an earlier time, possessed a detailed knowledge of Middle Eastern geography. "It

wasn't just the Biblical part of Palestine that interested me," he recalled. "The whole history of that area of the world is just about the most complicated and most interesting of any anywhere." That fascination was on display in the Oval Office, where the president stunned General Eisenhower and Undersecretary of State Dean Acheson, both of whom thought him ignorant of the subject, by lecturing them on the strategic importance of the Middle East while referring to his personal, dog-eared map.[65]

So it was that when Ben Gurion & Co. gathered to announce the establishment of the new Jewish state (no one knew what it would even be called), they tensely monitored any possible decision by Truman and the United States to formally recognize them.

As it was, of Truman's circle of advisors, only White House counsel Clark Clifford thought the president should recognize the fledgling state. Secretary of State George Marshall threatened to campaign against Truman during that election year if he chose to side with the Zionists.

Finally, Israel's first cabinet met at 4:00 p.m. on the afternoon of May 14, in a nondescript building near the beach at Tel Aviv. Ben Gurion rose to read from a document (written in Hebrew!).

Hours later, Truman sent a spokesman into a hallway to read a brief statement to the press:

> This Government has been informed that a Jewish state has been proclaimed in Palestine, and recognition has been requested by the Provisional government thereof.

---

65   Oren, *Power, Faith, and Fantasy*, 476.

> The United States recognizes the Provisional government as the de facto authority of the new ~~Jewish state~~ State of Israel.

With his own hand, the president had written "State of Israel."

Thus began a relationship between American presidents and Israel that stood many a test.

Until Barack Hussein Obama.

From the corridors of history, we hear the exchanges between Truman and Ben Gurion, Johnson and Eshkol, even Nixon and Meir. While each was a unique and complex relationship, mutual respect reigned. Even Richard Nixon, who was known to throw out an anti-Semitic remark or two, ordered his joint chiefs to "send everything that will fly" to rearm embattled Israel during the 1973 Yom Kippur War.

In the summer of 2014, Barack Obama ordered a halt to munitions sent to Israel to answer the deadly rocket fire of Hamas, from the Gaza Strip.

On April 18 2016, a homicide bomber detonated onboard an Israeli bus in Jerusalem. The ensuing fireball injured twenty people. One mother spoke of looking up through the haze of smoke in the aftermath and seeing her burned daughter nearby.

Though the Israelis are very good at responding to security threats—it was the first such bus bombing in years—it reinforced the point that terrorists like Hamas are still active, dedicated to fulfilling their charter of wiping out the Jewish state.

The next day, US Vice President Joe Biden, speaking at a left-wing gathering for J Street in Washington, made an incredible statement; he claimed that the administration experienced "overwhelming frustration"[66] with … Israeli Premier Benjamin Netanyahu!

---

66   http://www.cnn.com/2016/04/19/politics/biden-netanyahu-frustration-israel-j-street/

As has become common practice among Western political elites, Biden unwittingly fulfilled Bible prophecy by calling good evil and evil good (Isaiah 5:20). For decades, but accelerating since the doomed Oslo Accords in 1993, Western diplomats and politicians have never missed an opportunity to bash Israel, while giving a pass to the murderous PLO/Palestinian Authority, which has radicalized Palestinian society for a quarter century, much of it at the expense of the American taxpayer.

The entire Barack Obama presidency was spent undermining Israel consistently. As has been discussed, we don't have to look very far to understand why Obama has the worldview he has. Just ahead of the Jerusalem terror attack, Obama's former pastor, Jeremiah Wright, blasted Israel and called Jesus a "Palestinian."

America's official turn away from Israel is but one sign that the United States, the world's greatest experiment in democracy, will not survive the Marxist/Socialist underpinnings of Obama's successful attempt to fundamentally transform the country.

How did we get here?

Friends for Life

Except for a few rough waters with the Eisenhower Administration and again under Jimmy Carter, Israel has enjoyed a remarkably flourishing relationship with the United States from the beginning.

Few know that John F. Kennedy (and brother Bobby a decade later) visited Israel—or Palestine, as it was then known—in 1939. His impressions, all the more remarkable given the fact that his father Joe Kennedy was a notorious anti-Semite, are amazing.

Kennedy, then a young man of twenty-one, was a keen observer of human nature, and this greatly aided him decades later in the White House. During his time in Palestine, he formed views that would provide the basic foundation of US foreign policy in the region for decades. Writing to his father in 1939, he advocated pragmatism:

> I see no hope for the working out of the British policy as laid down in the White Paper. As I said above, theoretically it sounds just and fair, but the important thing and the necessary thing is not a solution just and fair but a solution that will work.

Apart from this, Kennedy admired the Zionist work ethic, and his warm relationship with David Ben Gurion a generation later would help the still-growing Jewish state move into modernity.

Of course, Kennedy's successor would prove to be a valuable friend as well. Lyndon Johnson advised the Israelis to stand down in the wake of Nasser's bellicosity in the spring of 1967, but there is no reason to believe he would not have intervened militarily had the Israelis needed it—even though his administration was already bogged down in Vietnam.

Publicly, Johnson wished to be seen as even-handed:

> The President indicated to [Israeli Ambassador Abba] Eban that before the United States took any forceful action, he would have to get a resolution from Congress. To Eban, this was waffling badly. For that would probably take weeks of bitter debate.[4]

We discussed Richard Nixon's positive response to Golda Meir's pleas a few years later, and we then move into the somewhat difficult Jimmy Carter years.

The one-term president seemed to genuinely dislike Menachem Begin and virtually forced the Israelis to Camp David. Still, it must be remembered that the "cold peace" the trio of Carter/Begin/Sadat forged in 1979 has lasted to this day.

Carter's bizarre meddling—and apparent anti-Semitism—emerged years later. In his 2006 book, *Palestine: Peace, Not Apartheid*, the former president used incendiary language even in the book's title (Israel is in no way, shape, or form an "apartheid" state, with Arabs holding positions of power in government, etc.). He also filled his book with outright falsehoods:

> Carter
>
> *Palestine: Peace, Not Apartheid*, Page 50: 'Perhaps the most serious omission of the Camp David talks was the failure to clarify in writing Begin's verbal promise concerning the settlement freeze during subsequent peace talks.'
>
> Fact:
>
> Menahem Begin promised in the Camp David discussions to maintain a three-month settlement freeze and he adhered to his commitment. This was dramatically underscored in a public forum about the Camp David agreements on September 17, 2003 at the Woodrow Wilson Center. A member of the panel, Israeli jurist Aharon Barak, explained he had attended the relevant meeting at which the settlement freeze discussion transpired, had been the only one present taking notes, and that his notes showed Begin had agreed only to a three month freeze.

Ronald Reagan of course was a great friend to Israel, even though the Israeli airstrike on Iraq's Osirak nuclear reactor (which saved Allied forces a decade later!) was carried out without informing the president ahead of time.

Cracks began to appear, however, beginning with George Herbert Walker Bush (my book, *Eye to Eye: Facing the Consequences of Dividing*

Israel, chronicles the pitfalls faced by America whenever she stood against the Jewish state). It was Bush 41 who threatened to withhold loans to Israel, unless Yitzhak Shamir would sit at the negotiating table with the PLO.

This led to the famous Oslo Accords, the "land-for-peace" concept that has proven to be a dismal failure in light of constant Palestinian refusal to live in peace with the Jews.

The Bill Clinton years saw more consistent diplomatic effort, as the president worked hard for an Israeli-Palestinian Accord, to cement his legacy.

George W. Bush appeared to be a great friend of the Israelis, particularly Prime Minister Ariel Sharon, and he bound the United States to certain security guarantees, if they would divide the land and make painful concessions.

In November 2007, President Bush invited Israeli Prime Minister Ehud Olmert and Palestinian leader Mahmoud Abbas to Washington for the Annapolis Conference. There, he said, "Achieving this goal requires neighbors committed to peace between Israel and a new Palestinian state—and I'm encouraged by the presence of so many here."

As usual, when it got down to brass tacks, it was Israel that was expected to make concessions, further shrinking an already dangerously small country.

In the next ten days, the United States experienced the largest flood in the state of Washington's history, hurricane-force winds up to 127 mph in Oregon, I-5 between Seattle and Portland was closed for five days, and a massive ice storm hit America's heartland—causing chaos, a travel gridlock, and over one million homes and businesses to lose their power. Also, the largest ice storm in Oklahoma history produced the largest power outage in that state's history. President Bush declared major FEMA disasters for Washington, Oregon, Oklahoma, and Kansas—and did the same for Missouri, Iowa, and Illinois.

These were two separate, back-to-back, $1 billion-plus disasters bringing the 2007 total to four billion-dollar disasters that coincided with US pressure on Israel to divide her land.

Notice I didn't say that some of the participants in this flawed peace process were insincere.

This effort on the part of American presidents, beginning with Carter, to intervene personally to put an end to hostilities, was still done in a climate of genuine friendship between the two countries. Even Carter's alleged anti-Semitism didn't unravel the unique relationship between the countries.

All that changed in January 2009.

B. Hussein Obama Assumes the Presidency

A totally new kind of American president strode onto the stage of history when the former constitutional law professor came to Washington.

Within weeks he sent serious positive signals to the Muslim Brotherhood in Cairo, Obama described this country's friendship with Israel as "unbreakable."

For myriad reasons—not the least of which is the newly inked agreement with Iran, which places Israel in existential danger—Obama has worked tirelessly to disrupt the friendship.

It seems to have begun with his bungling (managing?) of the so-called Arab Spring, when fighting between jihadists and regime loyalists in North African countries led the Middle East into a cauldron of terrorism, death, and destruction.

(At the time this book went to press, more than a quarter-million souls in Syria have been slaughtered, with no intervention by the Obama administration.)

Background of the Arab Spring

The seeds of destruction for the once-hopeful Arab Spring, in which it appeared millions of Muslims were throwing off the shackles of their tribal overlords/dictators (Mubarak of Egypt, Gaddafi of Libya, etc.) were sown years before.

As usual, Israel was blamed for the wider violence in the Middle East, a seemingly obvious absurdity, but one embraced not only by ME Arabs but Western diplomats and media figures, as well.

At an "Arab Peace Initiative" summit in Beirut in the spring of 2002, Crown Prince Abdullah appealed directly to the Israeli people:

> Allow me at this point to directly address the Israeli people, to say to them that the use of violence, for more than fifty years, has only resulted in more violence and destruction, and that the Israeli people are as far as they have ever been from security and peace, notwithstanding military superiority and despite efforts to subdue and oppress.
>
> Peace emanates from the heart and mind, and not from the barrel of a cannon, or the exploding warhead of a missile.
>
> The time has come for Israel to put its trust in peace after it has gambled on war for decades without success.
>
> Israel, and the world, must understand that peace and the retention of the occupied Arab territories are incomparable and impossible to reconcile or achieve.

I would further say to the Israeli people that if their government abandons the policy of force and oppression and embraces true peace, we will not hesitate to accept the right of the Israeli people to live in security with the people of the region.

As I wrote at the time:

Why was there violence in the first place? Arabs instigated violence and destruction, and Israel responded in self-defense.

The Arabs have oppressed the Arabs of Palestine who live in refugee camps in Lebanon, Syria, Jordan and Egypt and are treated as second- and third-class citizens.

Peace emanates from the heart and mind. Does Palestinian incitement and teaching Palestinian children to hate Jews help the heart and mind? Why won't Arab countries commit to letting Israel live in peace and security? They don't because they are committed to Israel's elimination.

Israel hasn't gambled on war for decades, but they have had to fight for their survival with the Arabs obsessed with their existence before and after they became a state.

As always, it is Arab intransigence regarding Israel that is the root of the problem. Israel is accused of forcing upwards of 750,000 Palestinians out of the country in the 1948 and 1967 wars (more accurate assessments of displaced persons at the time put the figure at no more than 10 percent of those numbers), yet the world is silent about 1.5 million Muslims killed in the Iran-Iraq War. Silent about the Syrian genocide going on now. Silent about renegade jihadi groups terrorizing Muslim and Christian populations in the Middle East.

Israel has always been a convenient scapegoat, though.

The Saudi Peace Initiative is just such an example, especially in light of the crown prince's comments above.

I attended the Carnegie Endowment for Peace in November 2010 for Prince Faisal's presentation. Besides the Saudi perspective that it's all Israel's fault, another theme began to emerge, one picked up on in 2013 by the American president: the world is getting tired of Israel.

At the Carnegie event, Prince Al-Faisal was on a roll.

Blaming the Arab-Israeli conflict for being the powerful catalyst for radicalization throughout the Middle East is total absurdity. Arabs have the habit of saying something repeatedly until they start believing the lie, or they are totally deceived from the beginning.

There were many Jewish representatives of Washington "think tanks" at the meeting that countered Al-Faisal's bold statements, so he wove and dodged with his answers.

Those attending were pitching Israeli withdrawal first, then normalization. The displaced Arabs of Palestine are the Arabs' fault, not Israel's. So the question can be asked of the land-for-peace groupies: Why were the lands seized?

Not only have the decades of conflict exacted devastating tolls on Israeli and Palestinian populations, but they have also wreaked havoc in neighboring states by spurring violence and inflaming extremist movements, Al-Faisal said.

Spillover into Lebanon: "The conflict has spread like a cancer across borders," Al-Faisal said. He noted the damaging effects of Israeli aggression on Lebanon, where thousands of civilians have been killed in conflicts with Israel.

In addition to the heavy death toll, the Shi'ite group Hezbollah has capitalized on Israeli interventions, he said. It has used the potential threat posed by Israel to mobilize its followers and consolidate its control of the national government, which has hurt Lebanon's overall stability.

Radicalizing the region: The Arab-Israeli conflict has served as a powerful catalyst for radicalization throughout the Middle East. Extremist groups have cited the grievances of the Palestinian refugee community as justification for acts of terrorism and political violence.

But resolving the conflict would substantially dampen the appeal of extremism throughout the region, Al-Faisal asserted. Therefore, Western democracies have a real strategic interest in achieving "a true and lasting peace."

It is this last noble goal that every American president invokes. We shall see that Barack Obama has also cloaked himself as a peacemaker, but is he, really?

As we have seen clearly, whole Arab populations have thrown off the false idea that everything is Israel's fault, but Obama has accelerated his rhetoric on that score, while also claiming a false narrative for the Arab Spring.

When he refused to come to the political aid of Egypt's Hosni Mubarak, Obama was telegraphing where his loyalties lie. The same was true with regard to Libya's Gaddafi.

Both these men were strongmen, to be sure, but they were also the only thing standing between stability and instability in the Arab world. Now that they are gone (Mubarak removed from power in 2011, and Gaddafi removed from power and killed, also in 2011) and the power vacuum has been filled by the Muslim Brotherhood and ISIS.

While the Middle East burns, Obama abandons allies and arms and protects the jihadists. There's simply no other way to explain this. The plain truth is, Barack Obama has checked off a laundry list of items to help bring the most radical elements of Islam to power in the Middle East.

Unbreakable?

From the moment he entered office, Obama has fed a serious personal dislike of Benjamin Netanyahu.

For most, the contrast in every way between the two men could not be more stark.

Netanyahu, raised on a Zionist ethic by his father, Benzion (himself a key member of the team that created the conditions for statehood), served in Israel's elite counter-terrorism unit, Sayeret Matkal. When his older brother, Jonathan, was killed leading the famous raid at Entebbe in 1976 (perhaps the most successful hostage-rescue of all time), Benjamin changed the focus of his career from business to politics. He has said many times that Entebbe altered the trajectory of his life.

Israel has benefitted from this.

At the same time, Obama heaped around himself radical Marxist professors, friends, and advisors. His sympathy for the Palestinian cause (read: the liquidation of Israel) began in earnest in Chicago. His deeply anti-Semitic pastor, the Rev. Jeremiah Wright of Trinity United Church of Christ, educated him on Liberation Theology, the joint story of oppression crafted by '60s radicals in the United States and Palestinian journalists and religious figures even today.

Obama's loathing of Israel also explains how he can obscenely criticize Netanyahu and our ally Israel, while at the same time claiming he couldn't "meddle" in the corrupt Iranian elections of 2009, when the mullahs in Tehran were teetering on the edge of collapse.

Prop up Iran, tear down Israel.

It is important to note, too, that Obama hasn't even a shred of biblical worldview. In fairness, the same thing can be said for scores of American diplomats and politicians, who have forced on Israel the disastrous land-for-peace formula. The president and Beltway insiders have probably never heard of Joel 3:2:

> I will also gather all nations, and will bring them down into the valley of Jehoshaphat, and will plead with them there for my people and for my heritage Israel, whom they have scattered among the nations, and parted my land.

Obama would no doubt laugh at the concept of divine retribution for breaking his commands, but the fact is, Western powers have set themselves up for divine judgment, based on "land-for-peace."

Consider the very small following sampling of anti-Israel measures and anti-Jewish though brought about by Obama:

- A reduction in the sale of "bunker-buster" bombs, which would greatly aid an Israeli airstrike on Iran's nuclear facilities.

- In April 2009, mere weeks after Obama assumed office, the United States allowed Turkey to provide weapons and training for the Lebanese Army, which had threatened Israel.

(In a remarkably bipartisan show of support to Israel, by contrast, Rep. Steny Hoyer visited Israel in 2009 and pointed out in a press conference that 368 out of 435 members of the House of Representatives had sent Obama a letter supporting Israel in its right to defend itself.)

- In August 2009, Obama addressed one thousand rabbis in Washington, attempting to gain support for his radical health-care overhaul. As Jews pray that they will be included in the Book of Life, Obama referred to those prayers and said: "We are God's partners in matters of life and death."

Except that no observant Jew would believe that. One writer at the time, Andrew Klavan, noted Jeremiah 1:5 and Job 38:17, in which the Lord's power and wisdom are seen as infinitely greater than mortal man, whom he would not "consult" for anything.

Obama blithely ignores such "blunders," further exposing his anti-Jewish bias.

It is with regard to Obama's dangerously matter-of-fact "deal" with Iran that one can see his callous disregard for Israel.

Haman 2.0

Bible students are familiar with the dramatic story from the book of Esther. Haman, a top official in the palace of the Medo-Persian king, plotted to murder all the Jews in the kingdom (this a few generations after the Babylonian invasion of Israel, in which the temple was destroyed in Jerusalem).

Eventually Queen Esther worked with Mordechai to thwart the evil designs of Haman, and the latter was in fact hanged on the very gallows he had built to execute Jews.

We are faced today with a very similar situation. That ancient kingdom flourished for a time in what is now Iran, and the mullahs in charge in Tehran have hatched the ultimate genocidal scheme to do what so many dictators could not do: rid the earth of any Jews.

In 2015 America, we have awakened to a reality that seems not to be reality, but rather a brutal nightmare: the American president and his secretary of state have just concluded a nightmarish deal that will allow Iran to continue to pursue its diabolical desire for a nuclear stockpile, with which they can threaten not only Israel, but also—incredibly—the United States, with a lethal stockpile of intercontinental ballistic missiles (ICBMs).

Stunningly, Obama has said publicly that no country should have the temerity to try and tell Tehran what to do, since all sovereign countries must have the right to protect their own interests. This in spite of the fact that no country on earth has ever had the right to exterminate an entire people.

Welcome to ObamaWorld.

In addition to his raising of the stakes to unprecedented levels (imagine Iran with nukes and the apocalyptic will to use them, something they made no attempt to hide), Obama is also inexplicably advancing the cause of jihadists around the globe. In fact, on a FOXNews broadcast on July 17, 2015, analyst Richard Grenell said that under Obama's watch, "ISIS has created a country!" which refers to the territory now under the control of the jihadist killers in parts of Iraq and parts of Syria. They are doing so with captured American weaponry!

Analyst Daniel Pipes has speculated that Israel has three options:

- Conventional airstrike on Iran's nuclear facilities

- A commando operation (part of which has already taken place)

- A preemptive nuclear strike, launched from Israel's Dolphin-class submarines.

Because of Barack Obama's deadly game, the Jewish state faces these options, in order to survive. Pipes believes the Israelis will ultimately choose the second option.

However, all my experience and sources in Israel tells me one thing: do not be surprised if Benjamin Netanyahu chooses the preemptive strike.

In such a scenario, Israel would become a pariah in the international community and no doubt face a serious uptick in terrorism aimed at it from all directions.

But Israel would be a live pariah.

Obama's Palestinian Roots

It's always important to "follow the money," to follow the networks, in order to understand why people do what they do. In Obama's case, his clear favoritism for jihadists, including Palestinians, comes from somewhere. He didn't just come to these conclusions once assuming office.

Stanley Kurtz has written a terrific book, *Radical-in-Chief*, which outlines much of this. It seems that Obama goes back a long way with top advisor Valerie Jarrett.

> Substantial evidence also indicates that during his pre-Washington years, Obama was both supportive of the Palestinian cause and critical of America's stance toward Israel. Although Obama began to voice undifferentiated support for Israel around 2004 (as he ran for U.S. Senate and his national visibility rose), critics and even some backers have long suspected that his pro-Palestinian inclinations survive. The continuing influence of Obama's pro-Palestinian sentiments is the best way to make sense of the president's recent tilt away from Israel.[67]

Now, note the ties to Jarrett and her own globalist worldview:

> Top presidential aide and longtime Obama family friend Valerie Jarrett was born and raised in Iran for the first five years of her life. In explaining how she first grew close to Obama, Jarrett says they traded stories of their youthful travels. As Jarrett told Obama biographer David Remnick: "He and I shared a view of where the United States fit in the world, which is often different from the view people have who have not traveled outside the United States as young children." Remnick

---

67   *Chicago Daily News*, June 20, 1967, page 9.

continues: "Through her travels, Jarrett felt that she had come to see the United States with a greater objectivity as one country among many, rather than as the center of all wisdom and experience." Speaking with the authority of a close personal friend and top political adviser, then, Jarrett affirms that she and Obama reject traditional American exceptionalism. One hallmark of America's exceptionalist perspective, of course, is our unique alliance with a democratic Israel, even in the face of intense criticism of that alliance from much of the rest of the world."[68]

Obama's empathy for the Palestinians, borne of an affinity for a totalitarian worldview, has many layers. The network of friends doesn't stop with Jarrett.

His friendship in Chicago with Rashid Khalidi (the Edward Said Professor of Modern Arab Studies at Columbia University) is telling. Khalidi is a disciple of the late Edward Said, former member of the PLO and widely acclaimed academic from Columbia University.

Khalidi told the Los Angeles Times that as president, Obama, "because of his unusual background, with family ties in Kenya and Indonesia, would be more understanding of the Palestinian experience than typical American politicians."[69]

Understanding he is. Apart from his animosity toward Benjamin Netanyahu, Obama undermines Israel in practical ways. His newly signed "deal" with the Iranians also places pressure on American companies to reinvest in Iran, thus adding one more revenue stream for the mullahs to finance global terrorism, including that aimed at Israel. Hezbollah

68   *Bearing False Witness* (CAMERA, Boston MA, 2007), 14.
69   http://www.nationalreview.com/article/268159/pro-palestinian-chief-stanley-kurtz

and Hamas will benefit from these investments, oil revenues, and the rollback of sanctions against the regime.

But with Obama, the aid to Palestinians and their financial backers goes deeper, into hardcore ideology. He believes, along with jihadists, that Israel was born in sin and is illegitimate.

In his sophomore year at California Occidental College, Obama began delving into anti-apartheid activities. (The modern linkage of past South African racial policies, and that of the Jewish state in its treatment of Palestinians, is a strengthening propaganda weapon, as scores of young people now believe Israel runs a similar type regime and oppresses the Palestinians. The truth is something quite different.)

Obama also took a course under Said during his undergraduate work at Columbia. This was at the same time Said published his influential book, *The Question of Palestine.*

Two decades ago, Khalidi attended a fundraising event for Obama's first political campaign, and this was held at the home of domestic terrorist Bill Ayers (himself a disciple of the Marxist Saul Alinsky).

A few years later, as Kurtz reports,[70] Barack and Michelle Obama attended a dinner in Chicago, in which Said spoke "on harsh criticisms of Israel, which he equated with both South Africa's apartheid state and Nazi Germany."

In this era, too, we see how Obama learned to silence political enemies:

> Presciently, Said's talk also called on Palestinians to orchestrate an international campaign to stigmatize Israel as an illegitimate apartheid state. So broadly speaking, this is what Obama would have heard from his former teacher at that May 1998 encounter. Yet Obama was clearly comfortable enough with Said's

---

70   Ibid.

take on Israel to deepen his relationship with Khalidi and his Arab American Action Network (AAAN). We know this, because Ali Abunimah, longtime vice president of the AAAN, has told us so. In many ways, Abunimah is the neglected key to reconstructing the story of Obama's alliance with Khalidi and AAAN. While Abunimah's accounts of Obama's alliance with AAAN have long been public, they are not widely known. Nor have Abunimah's writings been pieced together with Obama's history of support for AAAN. Doing so creates a disturbing picture of Obama's political convictions on the Palestinian question.

In late summer 1998, for example, a few months after Obama's encounter with Edward Said, Abunimah and AAAN were caught up in a national controversy over the alleged blacklisting of respected terrorism expert Steve Emerson by National Public Radio. In August of that year, NPR had interviewed Emerson on air about Osama bin Laden's terror network. According to columnist Jeff Jacoby, however, Abunimah managed to obtain a promise from NPR to ban Emerson from its airwaves, on the grounds that Emerson was an anti-Arab bigot. It took Jacoby's research and public objections to lift the ban. Attempting to bar an expert on Osama bin Laden's terror network from the airwaves is not exactly a feather in AAAN's cap. Yet Obama continued his relationship with AAAN. Abunimah himself introduced Obama at a major fundraiser for a West Bank Palestinian community center a short time later in 1999. And that, says Abunimah, was "just one example of how Barack Obama used to be very comfortable speaking up for and being associated with Palestinian rights and opposing the Israeli occupation."[71]

Such activities and associations take us up to the present time, as the American president's foreign policy views are informed by an anti-American, anti-Israel cabal. Friends like Khalidi so influenced Obama on the issue of the Arab-Israeli conflict, his every move at present is as if lifted from that script.

In 2004, it is reported that Obama told Abunimah to "keep up the good work" when the latter published a pro-Palestinian op-ed in the *Chicago Tribune*. This then was at the time Obama had gotten himself elected as senator from Illinois.

The president's warm views of "Palestine" are cemented. They are part of his worldview.

Which places him directly at odds with Israel, precisely during the lead-up to what one-day could be an Israeli strike against Iran's nuclear facilities.

We know how Obama will react to that.

The Apple of God's Eye

Barack Obama masked his hatred for Israel while campaigning for the presidency. Actually, the lies he told as a candidate ("We will always support Israel's right to defend itself") are stock-in-trade for most politicians. During the 2016 presidential primary race, several Republican candidates pledged to move the American embassy from Tel Aviv to Jerusalem to fulfill a law passed by Congress in 1995. In fact, every American president since Oslo has utilized a little-known clause that allows him to indefinitely delay the moving of the embassy—ostensibly this is done not to offend the Palestinians and prejudice so-called "final

---

71   Ibid.

status" issues. Never mind the Palestinians have done virtually nothing in twenty-five years to forge a real peace.

It is almost impossible in today's political climate to find a politician who really understands the implications of a reborn nation of Israel. If you look at a guidebook of members of Congress, you'll see that when it comes to religious affiliation, most are of a mainline or Catholic Church background.

In other words, they know nothing about Bible prophecy and don't care to know. This directly impacts how they attempt to force peace between Israel and the Palestinians. And it doesn't matter who is president, or who his secretary of state is. Warren Christopher saw the Arab-Israeli conflict the same way Colin Powell saw it: in purely secular terms.

There is and has been a disconnect between Washington, London, Paris, etc., and the truths of the Bible. Interestingly, in American history, several presidents have understood the specialness of the Jewish people, but today we are far removed from the character-driven presidencies of men like John Adams.

Obama's Undermining of Israel

From his choreographed speech in Cairo in 2009, Barack Obama has signaled to the world's most radical Muslim terrorists that he intended to cut Israel loose. In modern diplomatic parlance, this was called "putting daylight" between the two long allies. Israeli diplomats like Michael Oren sounded this exact alarm and were roundly denounced by establishment-types in Washington.

In the spring of 2016, only days after Benjamin Netanyahu declared that the strategic Golan Heights would forever remain part of Israel, the Obama Administration said the exact opposite:

> TEL AVIV—The Obama administration does not consider the Golan Heights part of Israel, U.S. State

Department spokesperson John Kirby stressed Monday night, a day after Prime Minister Benjamin Netanyahu vowed that the Golan "will forever remain under Israeli sovereignty."

"The U.S. position on the issue is unchanged," Kirby told reporters during a daily briefing at the State Department in Washington. "This position was maintained by both Democratic and Republican administrations. Those territories are not part of Israel and the status of those territories should be determined through negotiations. The current situation in Syria does not allow this," Kirby continued.

On Sunday [April 17], Netanyahu opened a meeting with the Israeli cabinet on the issue of the Golan with the declaration that "the Golan Heights will always remain under Israeli control."[72]

Lest one think these assertions are the product of a Bible-thumper, consider the following:

No previous American president has had so strained a relationship with Israel as Barack Obama. As Israeli Ambassador Michael Oren said in 2010, "Israel's ties with the United States are in their worst crisis since 1975 ... a crisis of historic proportions." Author and scholar Dennis Prager concurred, "Most observers, right or left, pro-Israel or anti-Israel, would agree that Israeli-American relations are the worst they have been in memory." In the spring of 2011, David Parsons, spokesman for the International Christian Embassy Jerusalem, said: "There's a traditional, special relationship between

72   http://www.breitbart.com/jerusalem/2016/04/19/
obama-administration-golan-heights-not-part-israel/

America and Israel that Obama is basically throwing out the window in a sense." David Rubin, a U.S.-born Israeli author and expert on the Middle East, put it this way: "President Obama is very harmful for Israel and very dangerous for the future of Judeo-Christian civilization." The author and economist Thomas Sowell asserted that Obama's relationship with Israel had been consistent with the president's pattern of "selling out our allies to curry favor with our adversaries." Political analyst Charles Krauthammer observed that Obama had "undermined" Israel as a result of either his "genuine antipathy" toward the Jewish state or "the arrogance of a blundering amateur." In October 2012, Israeli lawmaker Danny Danon, chairman of Likud's international outreach branch, said that Obama had "not been a friend of Israel," and that the President's policies had been "catastrophic."[73]

It must be remembered that the key to understanding Obama's mendacity for Israel is very old, and it is a mistake to assume he has not maintained the old ties. For a man who is a disciple of Saul Alinsky and Bill Ayers and Jeremiah Wright (who provided a religious veneer to Obama's anti-American views), he hasn't severed those old associations. In 2007, Wright was named to the campaign's African American Religious Leadership Committee.

These kinds of associations, coupled with Obama's religious views regarding Israel, show clearly that he has no affinity at all with the biblical reality that Israel is the apple of God's eye. In fact, he and his associates would mock such an assertion.

---

73   http://www.discoverthenetworks.org/viewSubCategory.asp?id=1521

The Iranian Snake

Can you imagine what it must feel like to be the leader of Israel or the leaders of Sunni Muslim Middle Eastern countries to hear President Barack Obama and Secretary of State John Kerry boast and defend their horribly flawed Iranian deal? It has put their very existence at risk—with no regard for Iran's past diabolical and illegal doings.

These two men—along with Wendy Sherman, the lead negotiator of the flawed North Korean nuke deal—are extremely unqualified and were desperately looking for a Middle East legacy negotiated with Iran.

For France, Britain, Russia, China, and Germany, their motives were multibillion-dollar business deals for their desperate economies.

First of all, Iranian leaders and negotiators are chess players. They are well trained and very intelligent. A former CIA official with twenty-eight years of Middle East experience told me three years ago in New York City that it is not by chance that the Chinese, Persians, and Jews have survived the centuries, because all of them are extremely intelligent.

Iranians are also very patient and have a plan.

Obama has all but ensured Iran's continued goal of Middle East hegemony—which Iran said would exclude Israel—and the largest global state supporter of terrorism in the world, the nation whose leadership has called the United States the Great Satan and Israel the Little Satan, will now have tens of billions of dollars available to aid Syria, Hezbollah, Yemen's Houthis, and its worldwide affiliates.

Iran already controls Iraq, Syria, Lebanon, and Yemen; is making inroads in Sudan and Afghanistan; and has much interest in Jordan. Its purported plan for Israel (as expressed by the ayatollahs and former President Ahmadinejad) is its total destruction through the use of missiles and rockets from Hezbollah and Iran's short- and long-range missiles deployed in Syria and Lebanon.

Iran's rapid advancement in short-range missile capability puts every Sunni country that borders the Persian Gulf at risk. As Mark Langfan has shown, 56 percent of the world's oil supplies border or are near the Persian Gulf and the Strait of Hormuz. Therefore, Iran could send the world economies to their knees in a matter of days.

Israel had been told to hold off from attacking Iran every year since 2012—leaving the inevitable future decision of having to strike Iran. (Note Jeremiah 49:35–39 and Ezekiel 38–39.)

New alliances are forming. Israel, Saudi Arabia, the United Arab Emirates (UAE), and Kuwait have trillions of dollars at risk, not to forget the trillion-dollar world economies. Israel's level of cooperation has never been greater with the Sunni countries—who will be more apt to rely on Israel for defense than the Obama White House.

Furthermore, Obama has given Iran a free pass with no consequences for their destructive regional actions, their role in the deaths of American soldiers, and their sponsorship of terrorism throughout the region, which has greatly affected Israel and the Arab countries. They will now have a $150 billion-plus windfall and have eliminated international pressure on their nation and military. Obama has helped consolidate support in a country that has paid a great economic price.

If the Obama-Kerry Iran deal had been defeated, it would have been an enormous blow for Obama's legacy and would have pushed the debate to the presidential race.

At least one presidential candidate, Florida Senator Marco Rubio, stated that the new president could simply roll back the agreement, especially by reasserting sanctions, which had gone a long way in crippling Iran's economy.

It must be understood, however, that this historically bad deal is a military strategy on the part of the Iranians, who possess ICBMs and would love nothing more than to eliminate American military might from the earth.

No matter what, Europe will likely go with the deal. The French are the most skeptical; however, the Russians, Chinese, British, and Germans seem content with the deal and the future financial windfall.

The Russian Bear

In late September 2015, Obama spoke to the UN's General Assembly, the same gathering where the Iranians and Russians humiliated him by flicking away his comments like a common housefly. Indeed, Russia's Vladimir Putin spoke honeyed words, then two days later ordered airstrikes against ... the Syrian Free Army, battling the diabolical Assad, Moscow's dictator-client.

To add to America's lessening role as a superpower, Putin then told the Americans to stand down in the region and to keep our jetfighters out of Syrian airspace!

To this, American Secretary of Defense Ash Carter merely said the obvious, that Russia's provocations were adding gasoline to the fire.

We already knew that.

As if all this weren't bad enough, news came at the same time that the Taliban had retaken the Afghan city of Kunduz—more direct fallout from Obama's disastrous policy of drawing-down the American military from the Middle East and Central Asia.

Thinking people, truth-seeking people, must ask why the American president is delivering regional hegemony to Russia and Iran.

Why?

Undermining Israeli Security

While still a candidate for president, in early 2008, Obama criticized Israel's conservative Likud Party during a fundraiser.

Incredibly, the president-elect's first call to a foreign "dignitary" was … the PLO's Mahmoud Abbas!

Events like these set the stage for Obama's determination to take Israel down a notch, or twenty.

No greater example of Obama's intentional harming of Israel's security came in the baffling Iran deal.

The president's administration leaked Israeli security/strategic secrets repeatedly in an attempt to shackle the Jewish state if it became necessary to strike Iran and prevent the mullahs from obtaining nuclear weapons.

Not even the Israel-hating Jimmy Carter had ever done such a thing.

Additionally, Obama's affection for anti-Israel types like Robert Malley (Mideast Director of the International Crisis Group) is not so well-known. Malley has long advocated a separation of sorts between America and Israel and has instead advocated for negotiations with Israel's sworn enemies, such as Hamas and Hezbollah!

In 2009, Obama also told CNN that he would "absolutely not" give Israel permission to strike Iran's nuclear facilities.

Also in practical terms, Obama has steadily refused to act as a mediator between Israel and her belligerent neighbors to the north, Turkey. The key nation, now headed by a pro-Islamist president, Recep Erdogan, has savagely railed against Israel in recent years, especially after altercations tied to the so-called humanitarian flotilla efforts by Israel's enemies trying to sneak weapons to Hamas in Gaza.

In a shocking breach of long-standing American foreign policy, the Obama administration in 2010 allowed the PLO to fly its flag above its

Washington offices, a clear signal that the president desired to advance the terror organization's agenda against Israel.

Of course, one of the best-known examples of Obama undermining Israeli security came on May 19, 2011, a few hours before Netanyahu arrived in Washington. , Obama had the audacity to use a speech at the State Department, to call on Israel to withdraw to the 1967 lines with agreed land swaps. A few days later, he stated the same thing at AIPAC prior to Netanyahu's speech. Such a brazen disregard for Israeli security (former Israeli diplomat Abba Eban once famously called the '67 lines "Auschwitz lines") signaled a cold wind blowing through American-Israeli relations. From the text of Obama's speech:

"We believe the borders of Israel and Palestine should be based on the 1967 lines with mutually agreed swaps, so that secure and recognized borders are established for both states," Obama continued.

Such public declarations have greatly emboldened not only Israel's enemies but also America's enemies, which are the same.

Finally, to add the point to our list of examples here, in 2014 the Obama administration told the Israeli government to stop assassinating Iranian nuclear scientists! That Israel has never confirmed its involvement with these deaths is further proof that Obama is not only not above publicly pressuring Israel—such a tactic has become part of his diplomatic arsenal against the Jewish state.

In my book *Eye to Eye: Facing the Consequences of Dividing Israel*, I documented how past American mistakes regarding Israeli security and negotiations have brought harm to our country. It is now almost terrifying to think what will be wrought from Obama's actions regarding Israel and the practical steps he's taken to undermine our great ally.

U.S. MILITARY'S CULTURAL DESTRUCTION

CHAPTER 4

ANY COMMANDER-IN-CHIEF MUST HAVE A VARIED SKILL SET: unwavering commitment to defending American citizens; resolve in the uncommon event of war; and the ability to stay on message for the American people in order to define our national strategy.

It is that last skill that Barack Obama especially lacks. It is but one indication that he is the ultimate subversive, especially when it comes to managing our military.

Danielle Pletka, vice president of foreign and defense policy studies at the American Enterprise Institute, in discussing Obama's overall methods, pinpointed the reason he appears so ineffectual as a leader:

> You resort to promoting messaging czars. The real problem is you have nothing to message. That's at the heart of Obama's problem. He doesn't have a policy or a strategy to message—not with the military, not with the political, not with the economic.[74]

---

74   http://www.washingtontimes.com/news/2015/feb/19/
obama-taps-rashad-hussain-to-combat-islamic-state-/?page=all

True enough, but we would argue that the problem is actually more sinister than that. Nowhere is that more evident than in Obama's dealing with the mighty American military.

If he is a true subversive, operating at the highest levels of our government, then Obama would first attempt to purge the military of competent (and patriotic) officers, including those who serve with the joint chiefs, and he would then cut troop levels.

Obama has done both!

A *Wall St. Journal* report shows just how far Obama is willing to go in these areas, and it also highlights the apparent inability of the current congressional leadership to effectively oppose him:

> News last month of the U.S. Army's decision to cut 40,000 active-duty soldiers, shrinking to 450,000 by 2017, drew fusillades inside the Beltway. Sen. John McCain assailed "another dangerous consequence of budget-driven strategy." Adam Smith, ranking Democrat on the House Armed Services Committee, fumed: "Sequestration and the Budget Control Act, which are responsible for slashing the defense budget, exist because the Republican Party held our economy hostage and threatened to default on our loans."[75]

The report goes on to note:

> The allocation of half the sequestration cuts to defense, at a time when it accounted for only about 20% of spending, was also President Obama's handiwork. In his memoir *Duty*, then-Defense Secretary Robert Gates writes that in spring 2011 the president promised that military cuts would amount to perhaps one dollar for every $10 of domestic cuts. But in subsequent

---

75   http://www.wsj.com/articles/how-obama-shrank-the-military-1438551147

negotiations, Mr. Obama stipulated that half of the $1.2 trillion in sequestration cuts come from defense.[76]

Bingo.

Obama's disastrous decision to pull American troops out of Iraq, leaving the region at the mercy of ISIS and other jihadist groups, directly endangers Americans and weakens our interests. The overall effort to downsize the military has far-reaching implications.

In 2012, Gen. Martin Dempsey, chairman of the Joint Chiefs of Staff, said that if sequestration were allowed to go into effect, we "would no longer be a global power."

That's what it's all about for Obama, relegating America from super-power status to something akin to a European country. Again, it's his worldview.

A muted military has global implications, of course, but let's first look at how this impacts the volatile Middle East.

Removing American Power

Interestingly, Obama's main goal in the Middle East seems to dove-tail with those of jihadist groups and state sponsors of terrorism: rid the region of the vaunted American military.

A report from WND and interview with Claire Lopez underscores this concern:

> … [Clare] Lopez believe[s] the Muslim Brotherhood has thoroughly infiltrated the Obama administration and other branches of the federal government.
>
> She also came to the conclusion Obama had essen-tially the same goals in the Mideast as the late Osama

---

76   Ibid.

bin Laden: "to remove American power and influence, including military forces, from Islamic lands."[77]

Lopez is vice president for research and analysis at the Center for Security Policy in Washington, DC, a close associate of Frank Gaffney Jr., and understands that a key fallout of the drawing-down of the Americans in the Middle East is the fact that without those boots on the ground, Iran is emboldened to pursue its goal of hegemony in the region.

Front and center is its pursuit of nuclear weapons, threatening not only Israel but various Sunni entities.

As Ruthie Blum has astutely noted:

> One thing is clear, however: his [Obama's] presidency has been paved not with failures, but with a string of the most successfully orchestrated disasters in history.[78]

The Purges

Just one of the aspects necessary for Obama to dismantle the American military is one employed by dictators down through history, such as Uncle Joe Stalin and Hitler: purging the military.

A 2013 report from The Blaze outlined the viciousness Obama has been using since 2009 to rid the military of not only technically brilliant commanders, but also those with high morals:

> Nine senior commanding generals have been fired by the Obama administration this year, leading to speculation by active and retired members of the military that a purge of its commanders is underway.
>
> Retired generals and current senior commanders that have spoken with The Blaze say the administration

---

77   WND article; Garth Kent with Claire Lopez
78   http://www.jpost.com/Opinion/What-the-axis-of-evil-owes-Obama-415420

is not only purging the military of commanders they [sic] don't agree with, but is striking fear in the hearts of those still serving.

"I think they're using the opportunity of the shrinkage of the military to get rid of people that don't agree with them or not [sic] tow the party line.

"Even as a retired general, it's still possible for the administration to make life miserable for us. If we're working with the government or have contracts, they can just rip that out from under us," he said.[79]

When Chuck Hagel resigned as defense secretary in December 2014, retired General Jerry Boykin called on the former Nebraska senator and vet to come clean with the American people about Obama's agenda for the military:

Retired Lt. Gen. Jerry Boykin now is serving as the executive vice president for the Family Research Council, waging war on those who would undermine the family, the institution on which civilization has been based for millennia.

But he knows the military, having served as the commander of Delta Force, running a task force that hunted down drug lord Pablo Escobar, helping capture Manuel Noriega and turning in similar exploits from Vietnam to Iran to Mogadishu.

Now he wants to know the inside story about President Obama's damage to the U.S. military.

From the man who was there at the table, former Defense Secretary Chuck Hagel, fired (or resigned).

---

79   http://www.theblaze.com/stories/2013/10/23/
military-sources-obama-administration-purging-commanders/

"Public statements made by President Obama and Secretary Hagel regarding the state of our military do not reflect reality," Boykin said in a statement released through the FRC. "Once Secretary Hagel leaves his position, he should speak out about the impact of the president's policies on military readiness as well as his feckless foreign policy."[80]

Don't hold your breath that Hagel or anyone else who has worked for Obama at a high level will come clean. In fact, there is strong evidence that the administration has effectively blackmailed General David Petraeus, the architect of the famous "surge" strategy that stabilized Iraq after sectarian violence taxed the ability of the American military to establish order.

Petraeus, of course, ran into serious trouble when it was revealed he had shared classified material with a former lover. In early 2015, the story broke that the Justice Department—managed by Obama's good friend Eric Holder—might seek charges against Petraeus:

The FBI and Justice Department prosecutors had recommended bringing felony charges against David H. Petraeus, contending that he provided classified information to a lover while he was director of the CIA, officials said, leaving Attorney General Eric H. Holder Jr. to decide whether to seek an indictment that could send the pre-eminent military officer of his generation to prison.

The Justice Department investigation stems from an affair Mr. Petraeus had with Paula Broadwell, an Army Reserve officer who was writing his biography,

---

and focuses on whether he gave her access to his CIA email account and other highly classified information.[81]

Congressman Louie Gohmert (R-Texas) didn't mince words about the matter, claiming that Obama was blackmailing General Petraeus over the Benghazi scandal, which should have resulted in a purge of the top leadership at the White House and State Department. Instead, Team Obama went after an American hero:

> Congressman Louie Gohmert (R-Texas) addressed the Benghazi scandal and controversy surrounding former CIA Director David Petraeus from the House floor:

> "This administration knows that Gen. Petraeus has information that would virtually destroy any credibility that the administration might still have nationally and internationally, so what else would this administration do but leave over his head for a year and a half the threat: 'We're going to prosecute you, so you better keep your mouth shut.' And actually, they know that just the threat of persecution diminishes potential credibility.

> "So if you wonder why Gen. Petraeus has not come out in the last year and a half and said, 'No those weren't our talking points. Somebody that created them needs to be prosecuted. It was a fraud on the American people.' He's not going to say that, he's got this administration hanging a prosecution over his head. What do you expect? I doubt he'll ever be able to say it without worrying about something over his shoulder coming after him. So here he is. He's been defensive of the administration. He's been a good soldier, said what he's wanted them to say. He hasn't told all he could say, and

81   http://www.nytimes.com/2015/01/10/us/politics/
prosecutors-said-to-recommend-charges-against-former-gen-david-petraeus.html?_r=2

they're going to make sure he doesn't, or if he does, he pays a heavy criminal price. That's where we are now in America.."[82]

Interestingly, former Defense Secretary Robert Gates took note of a personal difference between former President George W. Bush and Obama:

> Former Defense Secretary Robert Gates sharply questions President Obama's "passion" for military matters in his forthcoming memoir, and claims that practically the only time he saw that in the president was during his push to repeal "Don't Ask, Don't Tell."
>
> The former Pentagon chief said in an interview aired Sunday that he was "disturbed" by Obama's "absence of passion" when it came to his military strategy. But in the book, *Duty*, reviewed by Fox News, Gates hit Obama harder—and in personal terms—by contrasting his style with that of former President George W. Bush.
>
> "One quality I missed in Obama was passion, especially when it came to the two wars," Gates wrote. "In my presence, Bush—very unlike his father—was pretty unsentimental. But he was passionate about the war in Iraq; on occasion, at a Medal of Honor ceremony or the like, I would see his eyes well up. I worked for Obama longer than Bush, and I never saw his eyes well up."[83]

Another disturbing tool in Obama's arsenal against his own military (and one we will fully explore in the next chapter) centers around the gay agenda, which the president has fully supported for some time. A Family Research Council (FRC) head, Tony Perkins, a Marine veteran, was

---

82   C-Span, January 2015.
83   http://www.foxnews.com/politics/2014/01/12/
gates-dont-ask-dont-tell-fight-was-only-time-obama-showed-passion-for-military/

curtly uninvited from speaking at an event at Andrews Air Force Base in 2010. A report tells the tale of how Obama's immoral worldview has weakened military resolve:

> After pulling more troops out of the Middle East, people assumed the President's support [within the ranks of the military] would rebound. Instead, the repeal of "Don't Ask, Don't Tell," women serving in infantry units and on the front lines, budget cuts, hostility toward religion, and an openness to transgenderism have all snowballed into a deep-seated resentment that show no signs of letting up. And while our servicemen don't have to like the President, they do have to respect him—a dilemma faced by a vast majority of the troops ...
>
> Unfortunately, the spike in suicides, sexual assaults, and job dissatisfaction haven't stopped—or even slowed—this administration's race to fundamentally transform the world's most effective fighting force. Ultimately, something will have to give—and that something will either be the White House's politics or our troops' will.[84]

Improper ... Saluting?

When a tyrant like Obama is in power, he will not stop at any reason in a military purge. If one's brass is all polished, test scores are impeccable, or extreme promise is shown in, say, tactical battlefield decision-making, said tyrant will simply look down and say, "Your shoe's untied."

Whether it is or not.

---

84   http://www.frc.org/updatearticle/20150105/military-support-tanks-for-obama

In other words, Team Obama will simply manufacture reasons to get rid of our best and brightest. From a Frontpage story:

> According to military.com, allegations of sexual misconduct account for the firing of 30 percent of military commanders over the past eight years. That figure that increases to 40 percent when "ethical lapses" such as sexual assault and harassment, pornography, drugs and drinking are lumped together. But there are other dubious reasons why these commanders have been terminated, ranging from unspecified dereliction of duty, to improper saluting.

> One of the largest purges occurred on the last day of November in 2011, when the administration terminated 157 Air Force majors, a move the Chapman University of Military Law and its associated AMVETS Legal Clinic characterized as illegal. They noted that the Department of Defense specifies that absent extenuating circumstances, service members within six years of retirement would ordinarily be retained, and allowed to retire on time and collect benefits.[85]

World in Chaos, Obama at Peace

As the world goes careening off into oblivion, Obama seems at ease. It is a baffling contrast now noted by Washington pundits, talk radio hosts, and ordinary folks gathered around water coolers.

From my good friend Keith Koffler, of "The White House Dossier":

> Obama's perceptions of the consequences of his presidency are cocooned within the warm embrace of

---

85   http://www.frontpagemag.com/fpm/208736/obamas-military-purge-arnold-ahlert

fantasy. Beyond the palace gates at 1600 Pennsylvania Avenue, though, the world is beginning to crumble.

Here is the wreckage of President Obama's foreign policy, contrasted with the irrelevant musings of his State of the Union speech. When will the destruction be wrought here?

The answer to that last question might well have come with the September 2015 announcement by Secretary of State John Kerry that the United States, under the direction of the White House, will bring in almost two hundred thousand Syrian refugees within the next few years. This staggering number, so sudden in its dramatic effect, will most assuredly include ISIS terrorists, who are following the entering refugees, much like an NFL tailback puts his hand on the hip of a blocker, then accelerates into the open field when he sees daylight.

Just imagine what will happen all across America when ISIS fiends see daylight and move to attack the population.

Obama's stupefying decision to trade five arch terrorists for a US Army deserter in January 2015 caused repercussions that will be felt for some time to come. Adding insult to injury, the deserter, Sgt. Bowe Bergdahl, appears to have cooperated with his Taliban captors (odd historical footnote: Bergdahl "went missing" in June 2009, the very month Obama gave a green light to the Muslim Brotherhood in Cairo to unleash its hordes across the Middle East).

Bergdahl, held by the Taliban-affiliated Haqqani network, caused the deaths of other military personnel who went looking for him. Yet this traitor was deemed worthy of release by no less than the American president (even though true patriots languish in Iranian prisons to this day).

Why?

(In a tiny victory for true patriots in Obama's America, Defense Department officials angered the Obama administration by charging Bergdahl with desertion, no doubt frustrating his chief benefactor in the White House.)

Finally, Obama has weakened the military (by December 2014, military morale had plunged thirty-plus points under Obama) when he ordered the Pentagon to put women in combat roles.

When then-Secretary of Defense Leon Panetta announced that women could now serve in combat units, Obama arrogantly signaled that he was pleased with the decision, which reflects his broader worldview (and misreading of America's founders' intentions). In a *USA Today* story on the decision, Obama fairly chortled that his will had been imposed, once again:

> "Earlier today I called Secretary of Defense Panetta to express my strong support for this decision, which will strengthen our military, enhance our readiness, and be another step toward fulfilling our nation's founding ideals of fairness and equality," Obama said in a prepared statement.

> "As Commander in Chief, I am absolutely confident that—as with the repeal of 'Don't Ask, Don't Tell'—the professionalism of our armed forces will ensure a smooth transition and keep our military the very best in the world," Obama said.[86]

So there you have it; just as he has fundamentally changed the military by allowing/demanding homosexuals can openly serve, Obama has also put women in harm's way—a decision that was unnecessary, especially given today's technological advances, which place less emphasis on large standing armies.

---

86   http://www.usatoday.com/story/news/nation/2013/01/24/
women-combat-change-panetta/1861995/

From Libya to Lincoln, Nebraska, Obama has ensured that America's vaunted military will be stretched to inconceivable limits in the years to come … mostly from fighting the terrorists he has so readily embraced.

LGBT—HE OWNS IT

CHAPTER 5

Every single American—gay, straight, lesbian, bisexual, transgender—every single American deserves to be treated equally in the eyes of the law and in the eyes of our society. It's a pretty simple proposition.

—President Barack Obama, October 1, 2011

IN ALL OF HISTORY, WHEN A REGIME/CIVILIZATION AFFIRMS homosexuality, that civilization begins its death spiral. Look for yourself: the Greeks, the Romans.

America's death spiral began in the summer of 2015, when the Supreme Court narrowly affirmed that same-sex couples could legally marry. As this book was being prepared, a Kentucky clerk, Kim Davis, was jailed for refusing to issue marriage licenses for same-sex couples.

An odd scene played out in the White House around this time, and it highlights the fact that for all his purported support for the LGBT community, Obama is controlled by his robust ego. At a ceremony honoring "LGBT Pride Month," Obama was confronted with a heckler, later identified to be a "transgendered" immigrant, who shouted his grievances.

Obama had the heckler removed, saying, "Listen you're in my house ... it's not respectful."

Respectful?

How Obama manipulates scriptures to justify LGBT back and same-sex marriage:

He asks, why can't there be compromise on gay marriage in a society that has Christians committing adultery?

"For many practicing Christians, the same inability to compromise may apply to gay marriage. I find such a position troublesome, particularly in a society in which Christian men and women have been known to engage in adultery or other violations of their faith without civil penalty."

He completely disregards the seriousness of a major passage in Romans that speaks of homosexuality and sexual immorality by stating that the Sermon on the Mount is more representative of Christianity:

"Nor am I willing to accept a reading of the Bible that considers an obscure line in Romans to be more defining of Christianity than the Sermon on the Mount."

He is harshly critical of pastors and uses a false narrative:

"All too often, I sat in a church and heard a pastor use gay bashing as a cheap parlor trick. "It was Adam and Eve, not Adam and Steve!" he [would] shout, usually when a sermon [was] not going so well."

He called pastors sanctimonious for believing in what the Bible says about eternal damnation; he doesn't believe the earth was created in seven days:

"Occasionally, for my benefit, she [my mother] would recall the sanctimonious preachers who would dismiss three-quarters of the world's people as ignorant heathens doomed to spend the afterlife in eternal damnation and who, in the same breath, would insist that the earth and the heavens have been created in seven days, all geologic and astrophysical evidence to the contrary."

He mocked and criticized "church ladies" and "church fathers" to justify his mother's confusing beliefs:

"She [my mother] remembered the respectable church ladies who were always so quick to shun those unable to meet their standards of propriety, even as they desperately concealed their own dirty little secrets; the church fathers who uttered racial epithets and chiseled their workers out of any nickel they could."

What gives his mother the right to judge? There are many special places to worship:

"For my mother, organized religion too often dressed up closed-mindedness in the garb of piety, [and] cruelty and oppression in the cloak of righteousness."

He doesn't want an unchanging Bible but one open to new revelations that suit his agenda:

"When I read the Bible, I do so want to believe not a static text but the Living Word—in that I must be continually open to new revelations whether they come from a lesbian friend or a doctor opposed to abortion."

He is troubled that religion or faith doesn't allow for compromise or, in other words, personal control:

"At some fundamental level, religion does not allow for compromise. It insists on the impossible. If God has spoken, then followers are expected to live up to God's edicts, regardless of the consequences. To base one's life on such uncompromising commitments many be sublime; [however] to base our policy making on such commitments would be a dangerous thing."

In closing, no earthly leader has done more damage to the moral underpinning of the United States and the world than President Obama. He has been the world's leader in promoting the LGBT agenda.

Is Obama treating anyone involved in this cultural debate with respect? Even the gay lobby is a pawn in his overall plan to transform the country. And he certainly loathes the biblical worldview crowd.

When one considers the horrific milestones in Obama's Oval Office career, we can only list a few seismic ones before needing to look away:

- The descent of the Middle East into chaos.

- A downgrade in the US credit rating.

- Spying on its own citizens reaches new heights (or lows).

- The Supreme Court decision sanctioning same-sex marriage.

In a numbing minefield of missteps, perhaps the worst is the culture Obama has created that thumbs the nose at God's Word regarding the covenant between a man and woman for life. We hear the argument often that a president in effect has little opportunity to change the country.

I think that perspective is mistaken.

Reagan of course changed things in a good way, mostly in his returning America to a place we could feel good about. His inherent patriotic nature "rubbed off on" the nation's citizens.

In contrast, Barack Obama's decidedly unbiblical view of the world has created a climate in which great offenses against God are now daily routine. Nowhere is this more noticeable than in the wholesale acceptance of homosexuality as a life norm.

How he came to his worldview is quite a story.

Obama the Christian …?

We'll cover this in more detail in the next chapter, but one key aspect of Barack Obama's embrace of the gay agenda can be traced to his religious worldview. For all his contention that recognizing gay unions is "the right thing to do," Obama is just as wed to this idea because of his religious background as any humanitarian reasons he comes up with (and remember, it was only a couple years ago that his vice president floated a trial balloon by recognizing same-sex "marriage," and a couple weeks later, his boss followed with a public endorsement).

Obama's Muslim worldview is there for anyone with eyes to see and ears to hear, but it is his encampment in Christian liberalism that is most instructive. Now, the countercultural forces operating forty years ago (think Harvey Milk) have become mainstream, and even conservative evangelicals have failed to stem the tide.

Today in America, religious operatives (and that is an accurate term to use) have become melded with political schemes, so that the ground has been prepared for the immoral, anti-biblical gay agenda. Spiritual leaders like Brian McLaren, John Shelby Spong, Rob Bell, and yes, even Oprah have made it possible for Obama to "come out" as gay friendly.

It's a perfect storm of leftist ideology and aggressive homosexual activists.

Even major denominations, like Evangelical Lutheran Church of America (ELCA) and Presbyterian Church (USA), have been hijacked by gay activists.

Obama's two decades sitting at the feet of Jeremiah Wright and the United Church of Christ established the future president as a leftist in the religious community. That, coupled with an unrelenting media campaign to portray homosexuals in the best possible light (talk shows, sitcoms, etc.) produced a climate in which Obama can make watershed statements embracing gays and their diabolical agenda.

Remember, Bill and Hillary Clinton (who can forget her odious participation in "Gay Pride" parades?) did what they could to advance the gay agenda, but the time wasn't quite right twenty years ago.

The right moment arrived for Barack Obama when he ascended the stage of history in 2009.

Obama and the Transgender Agenda

In June 2014 it was reported in a San Francisco-based (naturally) article that Obama was the first president to reach out to perhaps the most marginalized of the gay community: the so-called transgendered. Obama was the first sitting president to refer to this group:

> President Barack Obama, who established his bona fides as a gay and lesbian rights champion when he endorsed same-sex marriage, has steadily extended his administration's advocacy to the smallest and least accepted band of the LGBT (lesbian, gay, bisexual and transgender) rainbow: transgender Americans.

> With little of the fanfare or criticism that marked his evolution into the leader Newsweek magazine nick-named "the first [pro-] gay president," Obama became the first chief executive to say "transgender" in a speech, to name transgender political appointees and to prohibit job bias against transgender government workers.

Also in his first term, he signed hate crime legislation that became the first federal civil rights protections for transgender people in U.S. history.

Since then, the administration has quietly applied the power of the executive branch to make it easier for transgender people to update their passports, obtain health insurance under the Affordable Care Act, get treatment at Veteran's Administration facilities and seek access to public school restrooms and sports programs—just a few of the transgender-specific policy shifts of Obama's presidency.[87]

These recognitions weren't the worst of Obama's advancing agenda. Did you catch that bit about hate crimes? America's first Muslim president is not only aiding and abetting our enemies within Islam; he is also mainstreaming those who weaken our nation's morals.

In the spring of 2015, on the heels of his recognition of transgendered people, Obama escalated his grotesque imposition of immorality by targeting the most vulnerable: America's children.

Social conservative organizations are now raising red flags after it was recently revealed that the Girl Scouts of America are allowing boys who identify as girls to join its troops.

In a blogpost published on the Girl Scouts of America webpage, the organization's "Chief Girl Expert," Andrea Bastiani Archibald, wrote of how the Girl Scouts exists to serve "all girls," no matter what they look like or their biological gender.

"The foundation of diversity that Juliette Gordon Low established runs throughout Girl Scouting to this

---

87   http://www.enca.com/obana-advances-transgender-agenda

day," Archibald wrote. "Our mission to build 'girls of courage, confidence and character, who make the world a better place' extends to all members, and through our program, girls develop the necessary leadership skills to advance diversity and promote tolerance.

"Girl Scouts is proud to be the premier leadership organization for girls in the country. Placement of transgender youth is handled on a case-by-case basis, with the welfare and best interests of the child and the members of the troop/group in question a top priority," the FAQ page reads. "That said, if the child is recognized by the family and school/community as a girl and lives culturally as a girl, then Girl Scouts is an organization that can serve her in a setting that is both emotionally and physically safe."[88]

Astounding!

This kind of mind-bending social change has come about principally because the American president is setting the standard for what is socially acceptable.

What makes Obama's aggressive social engineering all the more sinister is the myriad ways in which he devotes enormous amounts of time to effecting these changes. Take, for example, his meddling in a topic that is a flash-point of controversy that separates families, communities, and ultimately, the nation.

For some time, ministries and individuals who have left the homosexual lifestyle have advocated for "conversion therapy," whereby spiritual principles are utilized to move a person from the homosexual lifestyle to the God-ordered heterosexual model.

88   http://www.christianpost.com/news/girl-scouts-of-america-allows-boys-who-identify-as-girls-to-join-troops-opponent-says-policy-is-slap-in-the-face-to-christian-parents-139239/

That just won't stand for change agents like Barack Obama.

"Protecting America's Youth"

Stunningly, in the spring of 2015, Obama actually called for *the end of conversion therapies*! From the Oval Office, where he is concerned with (or should we say, should be concerned with) matters of national security, managing national disasters, and coping with budget items … Obama the Potentate demanded that those who help homosexuals find freedom stop doing that!

The liberal-leaning *Huffington Post* described it thus:

> U.S. President Barack Obama called on Wednesday, April 8, for an end to psychiatric therapies that seek to change the sexual orientation of gay, lesbian and trans-gender youth, the White House said.
>
> The White House statement, written by senior adviser Valerie Jarrett, is in response to a petition calling for Obama to back a law to ban conversion therapy, which is supported by some socially conservative organizations and religious doctors.
>
> The petition was started following the suicide in December of 17-year-old transgender youth Leelah Alcorn, who died after her parents forced her to attend conversion therapy, pulled her out of school and isolated her in an attempt to change her gender identity.
>
> "The overwhelming scientific evidence demonstrates that conversion therapy, especially when it is practiced on young people, is neither medically nor

ethically appropriate and can cause substantial harm," Jarrett said.

"As part of our dedication to protecting America's youth, this Administration supports efforts to ban the use of conversion therapy for minors," she said.[89]

Protecting American youth? Valerie Jarrett? Barack Obama?

They are consigning American youth to the pit of hell with their anti-God worldview.

Again, with much of the world burning down around him, Obama (and the Woman Behind the Curtain, Jarrett) fiddles with social engineering, in order to create the society he believes is best.

In a further assault on our youth, Obama's former defense secretary, Robert Gates—in 2012, Gates became the thirty-sixth president of the Boy Scouts of America—advocated for the lifting of a ban on openly gay leaders for the Scouts:

> Robert Gates, president of the Boy Scouts of America, on Thursday urged members to lift the decades-old ban on openly gay adult troop leaders "sooner rather than later," during a speech at the organization's annual national meeting in Atlanta, Ga.
>
> "I am not asking the national board for any action to change our current policy at this meeting," said Gates. "But I must speak as plainly and bluntly to you as I spoke to presidents when I was director of the CIA and secretary of defense. We must deal with the world as it is, *not as we might wish it to be* [emphasis added].

89   http://www.huffingtonpost.com/2015/04/08/obama-lgbt-conversion-therapy_n_7029648.html

> "The Greater New York Area Council, Denver Area
> Council, and others are taking a stand counter to national
> policy," Gates added, emphasizing that the status quo in
> the BSA policy *"cannot be sustained* [emphasis added]."[90]

Several questions come to mind after reading Gates's statements:

- Does Gates seriously believe the status quo that has sustained the Boy Scouts on this matter is best, as inferred from his state-ment: *"not as we might wish it to be,"* or is this simply window dressing as he helps transition the country into an immoral cess-pool? Leftists like Obama and Gates often use such language to fool the populace into believing that such radical change is simply inevitable. It isn't. Such change comes from the sinister change agents themselves.

- The status quo cannot be sustained? Why not? What about the status quo in any number of other areas? Can the status quo known as the US Constitution be sustained? And who decides what can't be sustained?

In this case, Robert Gates and his old boss, Barack Obama, that's who.

The President Issues His Marching Orders

The leftist worldview of Robert Gates, now being imposed on the Boy Scouts, is curiously forming at precisely the same time Obama is eroding moral in the military.

> President Obama, in a historic first for the Pentagon,
> has chosen to nominate Eric Fanning to lead the Army, a
> move that would make him the first openly gay civilian
> secretary of one of the military services.

---

90   http://www.christianpost.com/news/
boy-scout-president-robert-gates-stresses-urgency-in-lifting-ban-on-openly-gay-leaders-139409/

Fanning, 47, has been a specialist on national security issues for more than two decades and has played a key role overseeing some of the Pentagon's biggest shipbuilding and fighter jet programs. Now he will oversee an Army that has been battered by the longest stretch of continuous combat in U.S. history and is facing potentially severe budget cuts. It's also an Army that after a long stretch of patrolling Iraqi and Afghan villages is searching for its postwar role in protecting the nation.

Fanning's confirmation by the Senate, reflected a major shift for the Pentagon, which only five years ago prevented openly gay troops from serving in the military. The policy didn't extend to civilian leaders, such as Fanning.[91]

The *Washington Post* article above, in outlining this radical new priority for Obama, predictably editorialized, noting Obama's "commitment to diversity at the highest levels of his administration" and the Post's Greg Jaffe ended the piece with further editorializing that borders on propaganda, claiming that Fanning's appointment "didn't seem to cause a stir in the Army, either."

That's in the world of Jaffe and Obama. It certainly does create a stir in the military when generations-long bans on gays serving is overturned by leftist change agents who desire to weaken our military.

President Barack Obama shrewdly uses his interpersonal skills to create a favorable public persona with the help of the mainstream media, which have been very effective in helping him keep up his façade. Behind the scenes, however, Mr. Obama and his administration

---

91   http://www.washingtonpost.com/politics/obama-to-nominate-first-openly-gay-service-secretary-to-lead-the-army/2015/09/18/d4b1aafe-5e30-11e5-8e9e-dce8a2a2a679_story.html

continue to take actions that are destroying the foundations on which America was built.

As commander in chief, Mr. Obama told the top five military service chiefs to either assist him in ending "Don't Ask, Don't Tell," or he would remove them from their positions.

Additionally, his six-year Muslim outreach—having brought members of the Muslim Brotherhood into his administration—has made the lives of chaplains and Christians in the military very difficult. The chaplains have been told that they cannot use scripture verses about homosexuality or ones that put Islam in a bad light. If they do, they will be reprimanded and/or dismissed. They have also been told not to pray in Jesus's name!

Obama continues to be very determined to force his LGBT agenda and the false god of Islam on our military, while calling himself a Christian.

Never before has the United States had a president that threatens our nation's military (its morale and preparedness) more than Barack Hussein Obama.

The so-called LGBT agenda is but one of those methods.

Blackmailing the Brass

Obama's demands on the service heads is unconscionable, as evidenced by a WorldNetDaily article on the subject:

> President Obama told the heads of the five military branches to support his agenda of "gays" in the ranks or find another job.
>
> The stunning revelation came from Adm. Robert Papp, commandant of the Coast Guard, in a Jan. 8, 2010 session with cadets that was captured in a video

obtained by Buzzfeed under a Freedom of Information Act request.

"We were called into the Oval Office, and President Obama looked all five service chiefs in the eye and said, "This is what I want to do," Papp said.

Papp, who was to retire in May, said he could not divulge everything Obama said in the meeting because it was in private communications within the Oval Office.

"But if we didn't agree with it—if any of us didn't agree with it—we all had the opportunity to resign our commissions and go do other things," he said.[92]

One can easily see how Obama's threats place countless of our nation's military personnel in places of extreme stress … all because the Chief Change Agent wants it that way.

Also in Obama's cross-hairs are, naturally, military chaplains. His vicious war on biblical Christianity dovetails with his aims for weakening the military. Col. Ron Crews has said that promises related to the "Don't Ask, Don't Tell" policy would not block chaplains from doing their duty have not been kept:

We were promised that we would see no change— very little change.[93]

There are additional threats to the jobs of military chaplains:

Col. Crews, executive director of Chaplain Alliance for Religious Liberty, was speaking at a panel along with military chaplains and religious freedom activists during the 2012 National Religious Freedom Conference in Washington DC on May 24.

92   http://www.wnd.com/2014/04/support-gays-in-ranks-or-quit-chiefs-told/
93   https://www.lifesitenews.com/news/get-in-line-or-resign-admiral-tells-military-chaplain

The panelists agreed that the repeal of Don't Ask, Don't Tell and other policies have made it difficult, if not a punishable offense, for military chaplains to read passages of Leviticus, pray aloud in the name of God at a soldier's funeral, or preside over traditional services.[94]

Obama's agenda rolls on.

Target: Christians

In rolling back the "Don't Ask, Don't Tell" policy, Obama is being very specific about those he deems the greatest threat to his aims: Christians.

Those targets' jobs are made much harder by the bulls-eye on their own backs:

One of the items on Obama's second-term agenda is to root out traditionally Christian chaplains from the military. He sees them as bigots unworthy of conscience protections. Like Chick-fil-A, they don't uphold Obama's "values."

Obama's mouthpieces in the military have already blurted this out. In 2010, Adm. Michael Mullen told a Christian chaplain who opposed the repeal of the "Don't Ask, Don't Tell" policy that "If you cannot get in line, resign your commission." That same year, Lt. Gen. Thomas P. Bostick, the Army's deputy chief of staff in charge of personnel, said military members who dissent from Obama's gay rights agenda should "get out."

"Unfortunately, we have a minority of service members who are still racists and bigoted and you will never be able to get rid of all of them," he said, as reported by The Washington Times. "But these people opposing

---

94   Ibid.

this new policy will need to get with the program, and if they can't, they need to get out."[95]

A Policy of Intimidation

We must understand that Obama's full embrace of the homosexual lifestyle goes hand-in-glove with his obsession over biblical Christians. The strange case of Family Research Council's Tony Perkins is a case in point:

> Nearly four months ago, Family Research Council President Tony Perkins received an invitation to speak at a national prayer luncheon held Thursday [February 2010] at Andrews Air Force Base.
>
> It was not an unusual request. Perkins is an ordained minister and veteran of the Marine Corps.
>
> But he's also a vocal opponent of rolling back the military's "Don't Ask, Don't Tell" policy that prohibits gays from serving openly in the military.
>
> "This is not an issue of two men or two women in camouflage holding hands," Perkins said. "It becomes an issue of intimidation. It becomes an issue of coercion."
>
> Two days after President Obama's State of the Union speech, in which he announced plans to repeal Don't Ask, Don't Tell, Perkin's received a letter from the chaplain's office at Andrews rescinding the invitation.
>
> The letter cited Family Research Council statements—calling them "incompatible in our role as military members who serve our elected officials and our commander in chief."[96]

95   http://spectator.org/articles/34146/muzzling-military-chaplains
96   http://www.cbn.com/cbnnews/politics/2010/February/
Tony-Perkins-Uninvited-to-National-Prayer-Luncheon/

Using Christian Leaders

Oddly, the muzzling of Christian leaders like Perkins (and another favorite target of the Obama Administration: Franklin Graham) stands in sharp contrast to Obama's utilization of other Christian leaders to advance his homosexual agenda.

A little-understood front in the war with the gay agenda and our renegade president is his use of religious leaders (a concept developed during the reign of terror under Joseph Stalin in the Soviet Union. The Kremlin head would employ Western leaders in the religious, media, and political spheres that would help spread the propaganda lies that Marxism was a worker's paradise. The term fits certain leaders today like a glove). These religious leaders are nowhere more prominent (and willing) than in the evangelical community in America. They help the president further his radical homosexual agenda.

Take Andy Stanley, for example. The mega-church pastor who serves as a virtual CEO for NorthPoint Church near Atlanta is also the son of legendary preacher Charles Stanley.

In 2011, Stanley invited Michelle Obama to speak at NorthPoint, and his 2013 "sermon," entitled "When Gracie Met Truthy" caused a stir—although Stanley was able to remain insulated and protected by most evangelical leaders who should have denounced him.

In the "Gracie" message, Stanley put his communication skills on full display. He recounted a story of a man in his congregation who'd left his wife and family for a gay lover. In order to try and minimize the embarrassment to his family, the man began attending one of NorthPoint's satellite churches.

When an associate pastor phoned Stanley to say that the man and his lover wanted to be involved in a particular ministry, Stanley said no.

So far, so good, right?

Wrong.

Stanley pointedly told the associate pastor (and his larger, television audience, for they were the real target for his evolving worldview that sanctions the homosexual lifestyle) that no, the men could not be involved in any ministry because ... they were committing adultery.

Did you catch that?

Stanley took exception to the men being involved in NorthPoint ministry because they were adulterers ... not because they were homosexuals. Stanley's pointed silence on the gay issue was orchestrated and I believe, coordinated with the White House. Twice Stanley has been invited to pray at the president's inauguration.

In a wide-ranging dialogue with Dr. Michael Brown, the Charismatic leader said this about Andy Stanley and the gay issue:

> Pastor Stanley also said that the church should be the "safest place on the planet" for gay youth, which could be taken in one of two ways.
>
> If he meant that a kid should feel safe to confide in youth leaders or pastors that he or she is same-sex attracted, that's absolutely true. They should be able to do so knowing that they will be loved and cared for just the same—as they seek to follow Jesus and pursue holiness.
>
> If he meant that a practicing homosexual teenager should feel safe in church, that's absolutely false. That young person should feel the loving conviction of the Holy Spirit, leading to freedom and new life in the Lord.
>
> Could this be why Pastor Stanley omitted "practicing homosexuality" from his list of sins? Based on his comment that he met with gay members of his church,

asking them if they wanted him to include gay illustrations in his book on sex and dating, one should fear the worst.

Quite explicitly, he stated, "There is not consensus in this room when it comes to same-sex attraction; there is not consensus in this room when it comes to gay marriage. We just can't continue to look into the filter of our politics at our spirituality. It's got to be the other way around—and specifically when it comes to this issue."

He could not be more wrong.[97]

As Michael Brown found out, Andy Stanley has his own agenda when it comes to the homosexual lifestyle. And as a friend of President Obama, he has a large platform and bully pulpit with which to weaken American's biblical view of homosexuality.

Another son of a prominent evangelical leader is Jonathan Merritt. A writer for Religion News Service, Merritt is also the son of former president of the Southern Baptist Convention, Dr. James Merritt.

In 2012, young Merritt was "outed" in the media.[98] Since then, his strong progressive worldview is on display weekly from his writing platforms. Merritt's worldview would be much closer to that of Barack Obama than it would be to Jerry Falwell, who founded Liberty University, where Merritt attended.

Rising young stars in the evangelical world, like Merritt, are helping Obama in significant ways by pushing the progressive views he and his own mentors have long wished to foist upon America.

Another Christian leader who is working hard to advance the president's agenda is Brian McLaren.

---

97   http://www.christianpost.com/news/
andy-stanley-on-homosexuality-hes-really-right-and-really-wrong-139009/
98   http://www.advocate.com/society/coming-out/2012/07/27/
prominent-antigay-evangelical-blogger-outed-gay

The former Maryland pastor is now a bestselling author and in-demand speaker. McLaren routinely tweets and posts on Facebook his affirmation of Obama's latest nod to the gay lobby.

That McLaren's spirituality-driven "Christianity" is more akin to that of past generations' liberals is a testament to his ability to fool rank-and-file evangelicals, who often think he's one of them.

The same can be said of young turks like publisher Cameron Strang (*Relevant* magazine), pastor and author Scot McKnight, and Shane Claiborne, all of whom are much more in line with Obama's worldview than previous Christian leaders.

It no secret and no accident that publications like Relevant (aimed at the burgeoning "Millennial Generation") and writers like Rachel Held Evans and Jen Hatmaker—women who appeal strongly to rank-and-file evangelicals—are working to soften the image of the "embattled gays" who are struggling for equal rights in the Shining City on the Hill.

So Help Us, God

The cumulative effect of the takeover of media, religious institutions, and the political community has been bad for a biblical worldview in the country. After more than a decade of growing influence by spiritual leaders and meteoric political leaders, America does not resemble in any real way the country we all grew up in. And so I now return to this chapter's opening: the forcing of and eventual acceptance of the "transgender community."

They are Obama's people:

> The National Gay and Lesbian Task Force seized on an advocacy group's report on transgender military service Thursday to call on President Barack Obama to issue an executive order allowing transgender men and women to serve in the military.

"We commend the commission for stating independently what we all know: there is no compelling medical reason to exclude trans people from serving their country, and transitions would place almost no burden on the military," Rea Carey, executive director of the task force, said in a press release. "The President should sign an executive order to lift the transgender military service ban.

"It's time to finish the job on repeal of 'Don't Ask, Don't Tell' once and for all," Carey said.[99]

Interesting how the president can both give and receive leftist marching orders, isn't it?

Wallbuilders has provided an extensive list of ways in which Obama has been hostile to people of faith:

Listed below in chronological order are: (1) numerous records of [President Obama's] attacks on Biblical persons or organizations; (2) examples of the hostility toward Biblical faith that have become evident in the past three years in the Obama-led military; (3) a listing of his open attacks on Biblical values; and finally (4) a listing of numerous incidents of his preferential deference for Islam's activities and positions, including letting his Islamic advisors guide and influence his hostility toward people of Biblical faith.[100]

(We list only a partial number of items; for more, check out the Wallbuilders' site—wallbuilders.com.)

- December 2009–Present—The annual White House Christmas cards, rather than focusing on Christmas or faith, instead

99   http://www.cnsnews.com/news/article/penny-starr/
lgbt-group-obama-sign-executive-order-opening-military-transgenders
100   http://www.wallbuilders.com/libissuesarticles.asp?id=106938

highlight things such as the family dogs. And the White House Christmas tree ornaments include figures such as Mao Tse-Tung and a drag queen.

- June 2013—The Obama Department of Justice defunds a Young Marines chapter in Louisiana because their oath mentioned God and another youth program because it permits a voluntary student-led prayer.

- February 2013—The Obama administration announces that the rights of religious conscience for individuals will not be protected under the Affordable Care Act.

- May 2009—Obama declines to host services for the National Prayer Day (a day established by federal law) at the White House.

- April 2009—When speaking at Georgetown University, Obama orders that a monogram symbolizing Jesus's name be covered when he is making his speech.

- April 2009—In a deliberate act of disrespect, Obama nominated three pro-abortion ambassadors to the Vatican; of course, the pro-life Vatican rejected all three.

- April 2013—The United States Agency for Internal Development (USAID), an official foreign policy agency of the US government, begins a program to train homosexual activists in various countries around the world to overturn traditional marriage and anti-sodomy laws, targeting first those countries with strong Catholic influences, including Ecuador, Honduras, and Guatemala.

Through it all, Obama has been striving to introduce the one element needed to take down a great civilization: mainstreaming homosexuality. His efforts in this arena will ensure that his all-important legacy—the legacy after all drives him every day—will have as its centerpiece his attacks on biblical marriage.

Taken collectively, the examples I've cited add up to a horrifying, gargantuan display of overreach by a power-mad dictator who happens to occupy the Oval Office. I am continually amazed by people I come in contact with who have little real idea of the overall picture Obama is painting, right out in the open. The contents of this book are shocking and ultimately can be best explained through supernatural examination, which we explore in the next chapter.

FAITH ON HIS TERMS

CHAPTER 6

The Lord says: "These people come near to me with their mouth and honor me with their lips, but their hearts are far from me. Their worship of me is based on merely human rules they have been taught."

(Isaiah 29:13)

I am…concerned about a guy that believes he is a Christian and pretends to be, and says he is, and then does things makes it very difficult for people to practice their Christian faith.

—Mike Huckabee[101]

I N THE COOL, SHADED SETTING AT MT. VERNON, **where George and Martha Washington are buried, visitors can see abundant evidence that the first president of the United States was a Bible-believing**

---

101   http://www.christianpost.com/news/huckabee-muslim-can-be-president-obama-pretends-to-be-christian-makes-living-out-faith-difficult-146026/#O8smLeePTsmgG4df.99

Christian; the pillars in front of the couple's tomb bear witness to their belief in the resurrection, and in Washington's study, the Bible is prominently displayed.

(Never mind the fact that the National Park Service, in the gift shop, displays precious few books examining Washington's faith. However, the contents of the house and grounds bear witness to his abundant faith.)

Throughout the history of our nation, various presidents have practiced their faith in various degrees, which reflects the overall population. From Abe Lincoln's rough, frontier understanding of God, to Woodrow Wilson's austere Presbyterianism, to John Kennedy's Catholicism, to Harry Truman's Baptist roots, American presidents have generally given a nod to Christianity, at least, and some have been outwardly devout, if not misguided in projecting a biblical worldview (see Carter, Jimmy).

Even Bill Clinton talked of his discussions with his Southern Baptist pastor, W. O. Vaught, who cautioned him to always support Israel.

George W. Bush famously came to Christ after a drinking problem threatened to derail both his personal and professional lives.

Then, enter Barack Hussein Obama.

The nation's forty-fourth president is too clever to tip his hand (or put another way, to tell the truth) about his religious leanings. Officially, he spent twenty years as the famous member of a liberal Chicago congregation—Trinity United Church of Christ, led by the polarizing Rev. Jeremiah Wright.

What confuses many is the seeming disconnect between Obama's professed faith and his policy decisions, including foreign policy and his kid-glove handling of jihadists, whether ISIS or the CAIR representatives that frequent the White House.

How Obama's beliefs about Christianity are distorted and convoluted

In President Barack Obama's book, "The Audacity of Hope: Thoughts on Reclaiming the American Dream" (2007), you have the opportunity to read about someone who is very confused spiritually. Chapter 6 is about faith.

Obama's so-called Christian beliefs are very distorted and convoluted. He spins and discredits the Word of God through biblical manipulation and misinterpretation while supporting policies that are in direct opposition to the Scriptures.

His faith is on his terms. He has said he believes that there are multiple paths to God, not just Christianity. He believes that Allah is the same God of the Christian and the Jews.

He perverts man's desire to love or be loved as the central theme in his radical LGBT narrative, attaches it to civil rights rather than acknowledging that the behavior is a sin as it has been for the past 6000 years and uses the terms "marriage equality" in his defense of same-sex marriage.

He picks and chooses Scriptures that support his beliefs. He supposes that Christians who don't condone his non-biblical positions are hypocrites.

The Scriptures in the New Testament that are in direct opposition to his LGBT agenda (Romans 1:18-32, 1 Corinthians 6:9, and Colossians 3:5-7) have no relevance to him.

He used his mother's negative experiences with Christians; most likely having to do with her spiritually eclectic beliefs and behavior, as an attempt to discredit them.

Furthermore, Obama has shown much more emotion defending Islam and Middle Eastern refugees than at the news of Christians being slaughtered in the Middle East.

It is important, even vital, to understand the networks when analyzing Obama's effect on American Christianity. For him, the arena is merely an opportunity to implant his leftist ideas into another public sphere. Take, for example, how the associations filter down to American youth.

In the summer of 2015, Chicago was the setting for the "Justice Conference," in which evangelicals mixed with leftists to sell center-left worldview to Millennials. The Chicago Auditorium saw radical speakers like Cornel West rail against white privilege, and worse, and hundreds of young students applauded wildly. Involved in the planning of the conference were Lynne Hybels (cofounder of Willow Creek, along with her husband, Bill), and the Rev. Dr. Otis Moss Jr., who succeeded Wright at Trinity as senior pastor.

Plenty of Obama T-shirts and bumper stickers were on display by the attendees, and the bookstore was stocked with product that would dovetail with the leftist worldview of America's radical president.

Birds of a feather.

Obama is committed to supplanting Christianity in America, and while the president occasionally attends church and bows his head at infrequent prayer gatherings, there is little evidence he is a committed, Bible-believing Christian. From being the most radical pro-abortion president in all of history, to his sinister associations with radical jihadists (the Muslim Brotherhood is warmly welcomed at the White House, as are Christ-mocking entertainers like Kanye West), Obama actually never wastes an opportunity to marginalize Christianity.

I work in Washington; in fact, I'm a White House correspondent. And I can tell you that many folks in this power town openly wonder if

Obama is a Muslim. His barely disguised contempt for Christians (and Jews) is that evident.

During a trip to India in January 2015, Obama spoke to an audience at the Siri Fort Auditorium in New Delhi. At one point, he remarked: "They've said that I adhere to a different religion." He then went on to say:

> In our lives, Michelle and I have been strengthened by our Christian faith. But there have been times where my faith has been questioned—by people who don't know me—or they've said that I adhere to a different religion, as if that were somehow a bad thing [emphasis added].[102]

A God-fearing "born-again" Christian would never say such a thing!

And, after pandering to the audience by invoking the names of Martin Luther King Jr. and Mahatma Gandhi, Obama said this:

> And there is another link that binds us. More than 100 years ago, America welcomed a son of India—Swami Vivekananda. And Swami Vivekananda, he helped bring Hinduism and yoga to our country. And he came to my hometown of Chicago. And there, at a great gathering of religious leaders, he spoke of his faith and the divinity in every soul, and the purity of love. And he began his speech with a simple greeting: "Sisters and brothers of America."[103]

These are the remarks of a pagan, not a God-fearing Christian. Obama's syncretic religious worldview is far more in line with a global spirituality mind-set than that of a president who prays on his knees to the one, true God.

---

102   https://www.whitehouse.gov/the-press-office/2015/01/27/remarks-president-obama-address-people-india
103   Ibid.

Yoga? Hinduism? Adhering to a different religion?

What more evidence do we need that Barack Obama has used a thin veneer of Christianity as mere cover for his real agenda?

Still, Obama is frankly so powerful that establishment types —especially those running for president—hedge when asked the Question. Former candidate Wisconsin Governor Scott Walker appeared uncomfortable answering the question about Obama's faith:

> You're not going to get a different answer than I said before. I don't know, I presume he is by his comments in the past, but I've never asked about that, and as someone who is a believer myself, I don't presume to know someone's beliefs about whether they follow Christ or not, unless I've asked to talk with them. But he said he is, so I'll take him at his word.[104]

Another presidential candidate, former Arkansas Governor Mike Huckabee, has been more pointed in his remarks. In an interview with Newsmax, Huckabee took issue with the low tactics Obama has used to embarrass believers:

> Welcoming a pro-life, pro-marriage leader at the White House with a crowd of abortion and gay rights activists is as classy as hosting an Alcoholics Anonymous meeting with an open bar. President Obama should be ashamed of himself.[105]

Huckabee's remarks came in the context of questioning about whether a Muslim can serve as president, a hot topic after Dr. Ben Carson said that a Muslim president would have to adhere to the US Constitution (a trap issue for a Muslim president, who as a true believer would

104   http://www.charismanews.com/
politics/50843-watch-scott-walker-says-this-about-obama-s-christianity
105   http://www.christianpost.com/news/huckabee-muslim-can-be-president-obama-pre-
tends-to-be-christian-makes-living-out-faith-difficult-146026/

have to support Sharia law over the Constitution. Notice how many times Obama has circumvented the Constitution and Congress in ram-rodding his goals.)

Comedian Bill Maher, an outspoken atheist, offered up an interesting observation about Obama's alleged faith:

> Liberal comedian and Obama donor Bill Maher suggested in a 2014 interview on Comedy Central's *Daily Show* that Obama is really a "drop dead atheist" pretending to be a Christian.
>
> Maher, an atheist himself, opined that Obama only joined Rev. Jeremiah Wright's church in Chicago "because it was politically necessary."
>
> "He joined because he wanted to move ahead in the political world and of course you had to be part of a church," Maher explained.[106]

Evangelist Franklin Graham, one of the few nationally known evangelical leaders who appears to recognize the threat of jihad, and isn't afraid to say so, has said that Obama once told him he joined his church as a mere extension of his "community organizing" activities; in other words, for political expediency.

As a political unknown nationally in 2004, Obama gave a revealing interview to the *Chicago Sun-Times*:

> "I am a Christian," the then-Illinois state senator assured. "So, I have a deep faith. So, I draw from the Christian faith. On the other hand, I was born in Hawaii where obviously there are a lot of Eastern influences. I lived in Indonesia, the largest Muslim country in the world, between the ages of six and 10."

---

106   Ibid.

"My father was from Kenya, and although he was probably most accurately labeled an agnostic, his father was Muslim," Obama added. "And I'd say, probably, intellectually I've drawn as much from Judaism as any other faith."

Obama continued by implying that most religions are rooted in the belief of a "higher power" and that they will all take their respective believers to the "same place."

"So, I'm rooted in the Christian tradition," Obama stated. "I believe that there are many paths to the same place, and that is a belief that there is a higher power, a belief that we are connected as a people, that there are values that transcend race or culture, that move us forward, and there's an obligation for all of us individually as well as collectively to take responsibility to make those values lived."[107]

Let's be clear: a syncretic, universalist perspective is anathema to true Christianity.

Stephen Mansfield, a prolific writer who has examined the faith of several leading figures, and the author of books like *The Faith of George W. Bush*, and *The Faith of the American Soldier*, has also written about Obama's faith. *The Faith of Barack Obama* came out in 2008 and was revised in 2011.

The book provides at the beginning a helpful chronology of Obama's unusual life:

The Life of Barack Obama: A Chronology[108]

---

107   Ibid.

108   Stephen Mansfield, *The Faith of Barack Obama Revised & Updated,* Kindle edition. (Nashville, TN: Thomas Nelson, 2011), Kindle locations 89–94.

1961   Born in Honolulu on August 4 to eighteen-year-old Ann Dunham and Barack Obama Sr., the first African student at the University of Hawaii

1964   Barack's parents divorced when he was two years old

1966   Ann married Lolo Soetoro

1967   Barack and his mother moved to Indonesia

1971   Returned to Honolulu and enrolled in Punahou School. Ann and Lolo Soetoro divorced

1979   Entered Occidental College in Los Angeles

1981   Transferred to Columbia University in New York

1982   Barack Obama Sr. died in a car crash in Kenya at age fifty-two

1983   Graduated from Columbia University and went to work for Business International Corporation as a writer and analyst

1985   Began work with Developing Communities Project in Chicago. Began attending Trinity United Church of Christ

1987   Lolo Soetoro, Barack's stepfather, died of a liver ailment in Indonesia. Entered Harvard Law School at age twenty-seven

1990   Became the first African American president of the Harvard Law Review

1991   Graduated from Harvard and returned to Chicago

1992   Married Michelle Robinson. Stanley Dunham, Barack's grandfather, died

1993 Began work with Miner, Barnhill & Galland law firm in Chicago

1995 *Dreams from My Father* was released, to light praise and attention. On November 7, Ann Dunham Soetoro died of ovarian cancer

1996 Elected to the Illinois State Senate from Hyde Park

2000 Lost a congressional primary race against incumbent Bobby Rush

2004 On July 27, made the Democratic Convention speech that launched him to national prominence. On November 2, won the Illinois general election for U.S. Senate. *Dreams from My Father* was rereleased to wide acclaim

2006 *The Audacity of Hope* was released and became a best seller

2007 On February 10, announced his candidacy for president of the United States

2008 On November 4, was elected president of the United States

2009 On January 20, was inaugurated the 44th U.S. president

This official chronology by its very nature doesn't explore Obama's early years, but we know enough to feel comfortable in saying that Islam played a dominant role.

Curiously, in the first year of Obama's presidency, a Pew Research Center poll revealed that there was a steep drop in those who believed Obama was a Christian and those who believed he was not. In fact, there was a 14 percent drop in that particular poll!

(Sadly, in his book, Mansfield seemed to at best give Obama a pass, and at worst, act as an apologist. In his introduction, he wrote of the suspicion with which the American people held Obama, and shamefully, he played the race card: "Obama was of dark skin, from a darker family background and may well have been from the dark side spiritually. Any slur could be made to stick.")

The fact is, Obama has serious explaining to do regarding questions about his religious convictions.

Perhaps unintentionally, Mansfield offers a powerful and telling glimpse into Obama's alleged Christian faith in chapter 3 ("Faith Fit for the Age"):

> The conversion of Barack Obama, too, defies pattern, refuses to fall cleanly between theological lines. Yet his turning to faith was one fit for his age. He came as many of his generation do—not so much to join a tradition as to find belonging among a people; not so much to accept a body of doctrine as to find welcome for what they already believe; not so much to surrender their lives but to enhance who they already are.

> We should remember how Obama has described his conversion, the phrases that have played so often in his speeches and books. In The Audacity of Hope, he wrote that "it came about as a choice and not an epiphany; the questions I had did not magically disappear. But kneeling beneath that cross on the South Side of Chicago, I felt God's spirit beckoning me. I submitted myself to His will, and dedicated myself to discovering His truth."[109]

Not exactly the Roman Road (Romans 10).

---

[109]   Ibid., 934–41.

This description of his faith journey, from the man himself, sounds more like the gauzy, dreamy description given by religious leftists like Brian McLaren. It is hardly the testimony of a Bible-believing Christian.

Mansfield and some others have written of Obama's alleged Christianity, yet the weight of evidence is decidedly on the other side. Keeping in mind Obama's own words regarding his "epiphany," it should also be noted that his associations, from his college years, belie the faith of a person who is rooted in scripture. In fact, Obama surrounds himself with religious leaders, ranging from imams to his former head of the Office of Faith Based and Neighborhood Partnerships, Joshua Dubois.

Dubois, a thirty-something who pals around with liberal Christians and leftists, also networks heavily with Christian Millennials, many of whom are well-placed in media. In 2008, Dubois was the Obama campaign's religious affairs director. His efforts went a long way in garnering the vote from young people, most of whom had no real idea who Obama is. In fact, Dubois's own background is in the liberal African Methodist Episcopal Church.

Of the 2,658 people Dubois follows on Twitter, overwhelmingly they are liberal, syncretic, and pluralistic religious types (for example: "Million Hoodies," actor Jamie Foxx, Hillary Clinton aide Huma Abedin, New Age guru Marianne Williamson, and Attorney General Loretta Lynch).

Additionally, Dubois also cleverly networks with influencers among Millennial evangelicals, including: IF Gathering, Elevation Church's Steven Furtick, and Samuel Rodriguez, a leader of Christian Hispanics.

Point being, these networks are in reality Obama's networks, and they all add up to a religious stew that is poison. That Obama has been able to use these influential young people to win elections and fundamentally transform America is all the more sinister and calculating. These realities come far closer to revealing Obama's religious views than do a few public statements.

Then of course, there are the deeply troubling links to that religion of terror, Islam.

In her landmark book, *To Hell in a Handbasket*, Jerusalem-based journalist Ruthie Blum made an interesting connection when dissecting Obama's speech in Cairo, in June 2009:

> *"Assalaamu alaykum* [peace be with you]," he said, extending an Arabic greeting **only** used when one Muslim is addressing another (which the audience necessarily perceived as Obama's way of saying he himself was one of them). "We meet at a time of tension between the United States and Muslims around the world... fed by colonialism that denied rights and opportunities to many Muslims, and a Cold War in which Muslim-majority countries were too often treated as proxies without regard to their own aspirations. Moreover, the sweeping change brought by modernity and globalization led many Muslims to view the West as hostile to the traditions of Islam."[110]

Obama went on to fawn over his Muslim Brotherhood audience:

> To show that he was not merely an American Christian, but rather someone who understood the Muslim mindset and was heartened by it, he recounted, "... As a boy, I spent several years in Indonesia and heard the call of the azaan at the break of dawn and the fall of dusk. As a young man, I worked in Chicago communities where many found dignity and peace in their Muslim faith. As a student of history, I also know civilization's debt to Islam..."

---

110   Blum, *To Hell in a Handbasket*, 2095–96.

After waxing poetic about Islam's having been responsible for much of the world's mathematical, architectural and other innovations of cultural and scientific significance, he went on to laud its humanitarianism. … "Islam has demonstrated through words and deeds the possibilities of religious tolerance and racial equality," he said, adding that it "has always been a part of America's story… Since our founding, American Muslims have enriched the United States. And I consider it part of my responsibility as President of the United States to fight against negative stereotypes of Islam wherever they appear."

The stunned and exuberant Muslim Brotherhood-heavy audience couldn't believe their ears. To have such a champion in the Oval Office—one whose stated objective was to look out for their interests the world over—was more than they had bargained for when they prayed to Allah for him to be elected.[111]

There are several important things to notice here. First, Obama appeared to signal to his audience that he was in fact one of them. Remember, the Muslim Brotherhood is the spiritual heir of the Wahhabists of the eighteenth century, who sought to reestablish Islam as the dominant power in the region, with a view toward establishing a new caliphate, as well. Their lethal "true believer" status fuels today's most radical jihadists.

Second, surely Obama knows that his revisionist history is built on lies. Islam has contributed little good to civilization, while wreaking havoc on innocents for over a thousand years. Either Obama was employing the Muslim use of *taqqiya* (lying to obtain a goal), or he really is a weak and fawning leader in the face of vicious ideologues.

111   Ibid.

Indeed, he appears to be more of a pagan who enlists the aid of religious leaders in order to bring about the New World Order he is most assuredly part of.

John Chisham, writing at the New Downgrade (a reference to Charles Spurgeon's battles with liberalism in the church in the nineteenth century), said this about Obama and his religious supporters:

> I have often wondered, and have questioned my emergent and other friends who claim to follow Christ, how they can vote for Obama, who is radically opposed to life in that he is for embryonic stem cell research (where you kill a baby to harvest stem cells), and is for third trimester abortions (the murder of a viable fetus for any reason, including birth control!)
>
> I think that I have discovered the reason...They worship the same god of their own creation! This god sacrificed his one and only son so that people could follow their own way of righteousness and gain heaven! They follow the same marginalized god that will allow those who follow other doctrines like Islam, Hinduism, and even no religion if they are moral "good people" god will be impressed with their works and allow them to enter heaven...[112]

Adding further to the confusion are the evangelical superstar leaders/pastors/CEOs who give cover to Obama's sinister agenda. This extends even to Andy Stanley, pastor of North Point Community Church, near Atlanta. The son of conservative Southern Baptist minister Charles Stanley, Stanley the Younger loves to associate with leftist change agents at the highest level. His 2013 prayer at Obama's inauguration is one case in point. There, Stanley referred to Obama as America's "Pastor-in-Chief."

---

112   http://thedowngrade2007.blogspot.com/

Huh?

Stanley then had the temerity to compare Obama with Jesus wash-
ing the disciples' feet (John 13):

> The takeaway: What do you do when in a position of
> power? You leverage that power for the benefit of other
> people in the room. Mr. President, you have an awfully
> big room.[113]

Such "pastors" do a huge disservice to the church overall by condon-
ing the deceptive and confusing behavior of Barack Obama. The lure of
power is indeed powerful.

In short, Barack Obama's seeming Christianity is in fact a front for his
true religious worldview: transforming the West from a freedom-loving
community to a neo-Marxist, Islam-friendly "community organization."

---

113   http://www.washingtonexaminer.com/pre-inauguration-sermon-tells-obama-hes-pastor-
in-chief/article/2519242#.UP7wMKWSdQl

THE LEGACY: WILL AMERICA EVER RECOVER?

CHAPTER 7

Righteousness exalts a nation, but sin is a reproach to any people.

(Proverbs 14:34)

THERE HAS BEEN MUCH TALK IN THE PAST year on US President Barrack Hussein Obama's legacy. Those on the political left, secular humanist, and/or political progressives that have backed him and his agenda are speaking of his legacy in glowing terms, but the true legacy is and will be ruinous.

The United States of America will never recover from his and his administration's aggressive assault on Judeo-Christian values and the great damage done to the nation's foundation. This has been a relentless attack in every area that is important to God-fearing and God-believing Christians and Jews. Never before has there been a domestic agenda as we have experienced the past seven and a half years.

The Obama legacy—in this chapter, we will expound on some of these:

- Undermined America's judicial system
- Ran roughshod over the US Constitution
- World's lead promoter of lesbian, gay, bisexual, transgender (LGBT)
- Leaving America deeply divided over LGBT, race relations, and immigration
- Destructive transformation of the US military
- Lectured God-fearing Christians on how to behave
- A Muslim apologist and endorser of Islam in America
- Passionate about Middle East refuges coming to America
- Showed no emotion over Christians being persecuted and slaughtered
- Endangered Israel and Middle East allies by destabilizing the region
- US federal debt will almost double to $20 trillion before leaving office
- Spied on Congress
- Promoted a false global warming narrative
- And much more

Undermined America's Judicial System and Ran Roughshod over the US Constitution

One of the striking things about the presidential primaries of 2015–16 was the label affixed to Texas Senator Ted Cruz: "Constitutionalist."

Cruz, a graduate of Princeton and Harvard Law School, was also associate deputy attorney general of the US Department of Justice.

The thing that makes Cruz something of a media story for this reason alone is the fact that a presidential candidate or president being a constitutionalist seems almost bizarre in this day and age.

Don't forget, Obama taught constitutional law at the University of Chicago, but he has done more to undermine the Constitution than any other president. He's gone about this in several ways.

Executive Fiat

Officially titled the Affordable Health Care for America Act (HR 3962), "Obama Care" was wildly unpopular when the first-term president set the stage his first year in office.

(By the way, remember when then-President George W. Bush floated the trial balloon of privatizing social security? The big idea never got off the ground. It serves as the mirror opposite of Obama's relatively smooth sailing to force Obama Care on the country.)

In order to ensure this socialized medicine gambit, Obama simply ran roughshod over the Constitution, forcing the issue on a weak Congress and an incredulous country. His famous phrase, "If you like your current doctor, you can keep your doctor," quickly became an obvious lie, as thousands of doctors retired early, sought ways to circumvent this new bureaucratic method of payment, or weren't included health plans' in-network approved doctors.

Although many mistakenly believed Obama Care would be free, it was quickly realized that premiums and deductibles would skyrocket. Obama then successfully used the Treasury Department to ensure that taxpayers (the 55 percent who actually pay federal income tax in this country) would be charged a penalty, should they decide not to participate in the new health insurance coverage.

It will also be long remembered that Supreme Court Justice John Roberts provided the tie-breaking vote in the proceedings to determine if the Health Care Act would prevail. This is another example of Obama using political pressure to exact legal outcomes.

That was just the beginning of the former law professor's mangling of the judicial system.

Appointed Judges

We err if we focus only on Obama's obvious desires to stack the Supreme Court with perhaps two new appointments before he leaves office (the untimely death of Antonin Scalia paved the way for Obama to immediately nominate a liberal judge, Merrick Garland).

His appointments of judges at lower levels are actually just as important.

Here's a frightening statistic: As of 2015, Obama had nominated over three hundred federal judges. Does anyone want to guess their overall political leaning? Only the most naïve would assume that a judge—who is a human being with feelings and emotions, of course—would be able or willing to consistently rule based only on what the Constitution allows. For decades, but greatly accelerating in the past few years, liberal judges have allowed their leftist bias to show, such as in the case of Terri Schiavo, whose feeding tube was removed on orders of a judge, while her horrified family looked on.

Of Obama's nominations, a staggeringly weak Congress confirmed 307!

(There are a few examples of Obama's social engineering with the court system failing. In 2010, Edward C. DuMont was nominated to the Federal Circuit. If he'd been confirmed, he would have been the nation's first openly gay US Appeals Court judge. A Senate pushback led to DuMont requesting that his nomination be withdrawn.)

In 2013, Obama nominated several judges for the US Court of Appeals. These went through, with Sen. Harry Reid leading an effort to change to confirmation rules. This is an example of Obama using his allies in the political arena to win with appointments that will advance a leftist agenda.

Obama in Our Bathrooms

Perhaps the most outrageous example of the president interfering in the judicial system and flaunting his blatant disregard for the Constitution has come in his strong-arm tactics regarding the so-called bathroom laws passed by North Carolina and Mississippi. This comes on the heels of another signal that our society is collapsing: in order to accommodate the less than 1 percent of the population identifying as "transgender," activist groups and some courts are forcing public companies to allow persons of opposite gender to use restrooms.

Incredibly, during a visit with British Prime Minister David Cameron in the Spring of 2016, Obama said the laws passed in those states are "wrong"(!) and he wanted to see them overturned.

> "I also think that the laws that have been passed there are wrong and should be overturned, and they're in response to politics," he said.

> Although the state laws were passed by "good people," he said he disagreed with their arguments.

> "Although I respect their different viewpoints, I think it's very important for us not to send signals that anybody is treated differently," he said.

> He described the new state laws as examples of local governments passing laws that are not "reflective"

of the national views on the issue of which bathroom a transgender person could lawfully use.[114]

This is executive overreach on a grand scale and signals troubling days ahead. Further, I believe the president knows he is wrong when he asserts that the "laws are not reflective of the national views on the issue," and he is simply attempting to create a different reality. Truly, he has used his bully pulpit for evil. For a US president to insert himself so aggressively into the law is something the likes of which we have never seen.

The LGBT Storm: World's Lead Promoter of Lesbian, Gay, Bisexual, Transgender (LGBT)

LGBTQ Intimidating Those Who Have Christian Convictions

The government, judicial, legislative, education, entertainment, and media arenas are attempting to push agendas that will force all citizens to accept same-sex marriage and related sexual perversions or be penalized.

Historically, America has strived to ensure religious freedom. Under Obama, however, under the covering of civil rights, the powers to be have pushed for legislative approval of all types of sexual relationships that used to be considered "sinful."

Christians are called intolerant if they object or fight the LGBTQ narrative. State leaders have been intimidated and threatened by the US government, corporations, and/or sports leagues to comply or pay the price in lost business. A relentless pro-LGBTQ media that has been infiltrated by activists supports them.

In the past, this lifestyle was not displayed in the public. Rather, it was kept behind closed doors. But now, its backers are demanding

114   http://www.breitbart.com/big-government/2016/04/22/ obama-bathroom-laws-north-carolina-mississippi-wrong/

approval and acceptance. They have zero tolerance for those who oppose the lifestyle.

Many in the media reprimanded those who opposed the Obamacare directive on contraceptives, sterilization, and abortion-inducing
drugs.

This is a very bad situation that is getting worse by the day. The next
step will be to attempt to penalize those who speak against it.

One of the things an American president has at his disposal is the
bully pulpit. With it, he has a certain moral direction he can go in, thus
nudging the country in a more conservative or liberal direction.

Past notable examples include Franklin Roosevelt's famous and far-
reaching entitlement programs, set on a fast track a generation later
with another Democrat, Lyndon Johnson.

On the conservative side, Ronald Reagan's ascension to the highest
office in the land brought about a noticeable (though temporary) swing
back to the right, on a range of issues.

Barack Obama, a clear product of leftist ideology, has worked tirelessly to fundamentally change America, and he's used every tool/
weapon at his disposal, including the media.

In February 2016, Obama appeared on the TV talk show *Ellen*, hosted by lesbian Ellen DeGeneres. The latter has steadily gained fame over
the years, using her witty, affable demeanor to advocate for gay rights.
In fact, millions of Christians watch her show and apparently see nothing wrong with it, which is one reason the country is in the shape it's in
(but that's a topic for another day).

Such appearances and associations have helped Obama set the
(im)moral tone for his presidency. Who can forget a few years ago in
May 2012 when trotted out Joe Biden, a Roman Catholic, who publicly
pledged his support for gay rights. When that trail balloon sailed off into

the bright sunshine, Obama knew his day for fundamental change had come. He pledged his own support for gay rights only days later.

Gay rights advocates and activists have made incremental progress in this country, since the days of very quiet gay lifestyles of Hollywood actors and actresses, to today's open and wide acceptance of the homosexual lifestyle. We are even seeing those who identify as evangelical pastors appearing to support the lifestyle, or at least paving the way for it. These include Andy Stanley, Carl Lenz, Brian McLaren, retired Bishop Gene Robinson, and Tony Campolo. Not surprisingly, these members of the clergy are also often invited to the White House.

But America has recently hurtled over the cliff on this issue. Three decades ago, there was both sadness and revulsion when it was announced publicly that manly actor Rock Hudson had AIDS and had long suppressed an active gay lifestyle. Even a brief marriage early in his career was simply a sham to avoid any type of stories coming out.

Today, the same situation would elicit massive declarations of sorrow from the American public. In effect, America has now embraced homosexuality officially. In the past, all civilizations that do so then begin a slow descent into oblivion. Not that that matters to today's instant-gratification culture.

Presidential candidates like Hillary Clinton also openly advocate for the so-called LGBT rights.

Destructive Transformation of the US Military

As he races to the end of his term in office, Obama continues working to undermine the military:

> In another historical moment for the Obama administration, the Senate on Tuesday evening, May 17, 2016 confirmed the long-stalled nomination of Eric Fanning to be Army secretary.

Fanning thus becomes the first openly gay leader of any U.S. military service—a milestone not lost on gay rights groups and coming five years after the repeal of "don't ask, don't tell," which had prohibited gay and lesbian service members from being open about the sexuality.

"Eric Fanning's historic confirmation today as Secretary of the U.S. Army is a demonstration of the continued progress towards fairness and equality in our nation's armed forces," Human Rights Campaign President Chad Griffin said in a statement.[115]

Admiral James A. Lyon (ret.) is another who has seen Obama's destruction firsthand:

There is no question that America's worldwide leadership; power and influence have been significantly degraded over the last seven and a half years. The basic reason, regretfully, is that President Obama has been very successful in the implementation of his goal to fundamentally transform America.

In so doing, he has undercut the Judeo-Christian foundation of this great country while at the same time promoting the advancement of Islam throughout our society—including the US military. Clearly, any thinking American understands that this transformation, at its core, is anti-American and anti-Western. Yet it is also pro-Islam, pro-Iranian and pro-Muslim Brotherhood. Compounding this travesty is Mr. Obama's decision to embrace our sworn enemies. Unbelievable.

---

115   http://www.nbcnews.com/news/us-news/
first-openly-gay-army-secretary-confirmed-n575661

When you want to take a country down, first you neutralize its military capability in multiple ways:

- Evisceration of the US Navy by Secretary Ray Mabus

- Relentless transformation of the military while ignoring the instability and worldwide threats we face has not only been dangerous, it has jeopardized our national security.

- Our force levels have been diminished to levels not seen since prior to World War II. In the US Navy's case, levels such as these have not been seen since World War I. This unilateral disarmament is being done under the guise of sequestration, an Obama administration initiative.

- The all-volunteer force is being decimated by forcing out tens of thousands of well-qualified male personnel under the guise of diversity.

- One of the first "cultural" norms attacked was to destroy the moral underpinnings of the military by the removal of the "Don't Ask, Don't Tell" mandate. The propaganda statements by Secretary of Defense Ash Carter that this transformation has been a great success are nonsense! In 2014, there were over 10,000 "reported" unwarranted male-on-male advances. If the Mr. Carter thinks this is a great success, I'd hate to see what he thinks failure looks like.

- Compounding this travesty is Mr. Carter's decision to allow "transgender" members of the military to serve openly starting this year. This is unconscionable.

- All of these debilitating social engineering directives are being imposed by people who, for the most part, have never served in the military and never will.

- The "multicultural" makeover of our military threatens to undermine the very fabric of our military forces, and is being accelerated with no apparent opposition from our military or congressional leaders.

- Obama has used the military's founding principle of civilian control to impose his debilitating directives, which are destroying the military's warrior mentality and the "will to win." As Mr. [Craig, Air Force historian] Luther stated, the objective appears to be that of a complete irreversible cultural transformation of our military.

- Those who remain silent are complicit with the transformation and destruction of our military forces. They are violating their oath of office.[116]

Destabilizing the Middle East

Obama's handling of the Mideast since 2009 is no coincidence, and it is not the work of a bungler.

The overarching question in "The Obama Doctrine" is whether Obama was right to reduce America's "overextension" in the Middle

---

116   http://www.washingtontimes.com/news/2016/may/8/
james-a-lyons-obama-lessened-us-military-culture/

East, as White House aide Ben Rhodes puts it. Obama reasoned that the Middle East "is no longer terribly important to American interests," that there's "little an American president can do to make it a better place" and that American meddling leads to the deaths of our soldiers and "the eventual hemorrhaging of US credibility and power."

As longtime Middle East observer David Ignatious of the *Washington Post* stated:

> Obama was wrong on all three, in my view: The Middle East does matter; the United States can help, and not doing so hurts our global standing. But even if he's right, he needs to reckon better with one clear lesson of his presidency: As the United States stepped back in the Middle East, others stepped forward. Russia has moved into the vacuum left by retreating American power; so has Iran; so has Saudi Arabia; so has the Islamic State.[117]

Spying on Congress

Incredibly, Obama gets away with things former presidents were excoriated over. Consider the administration's outrageous spying on members of Congress:

> Lawmakers are demanding that the Obama administration disclose how it used private communications that were intercepted during a massive spy operation on Israel that included private conversations with members of Congress, according to letters sent to the National Security Agency and White House.
>
> Rep. Ron DeSantis (R., Fla.) petitioned President Barack Obama late Monday afternoon, demanding the administration reveal how it used information obtained

---

117   https://www.washingtonpost.com/blogs/post-partisan/wp/2016/03/15/
obamas-destabilizing-candor-on-the-middle-east/

during secret surveillance of Israeli leaders, according to a copy of the letter obtained by the Washington Free Beacon.

Reports emerged last week that the NSA's spy operation picked up private communications between Israeli officials, members of Congress, and U.S. Jewish community leaders. The information reportedly centered on Israeli efforts to halt the nuclear negotiations. The White House reportedly did not take steps to ensure that these political conversations were omitted.

DeSantis, who along with several other lawmakers has already requested that the NSA provide Congress with details of the operation, informed the Obama administration late Monday that he is seeking to learn if the information gleaned from these private conversations was used by the White House to sway the national debate over the Iran nuclear agreement.

"I am concerned that the vague guidelines and policies used by the NSA for intelligence collection and sharing, in conjunction with elusive direction from the Administration, have led to intelligence being collected on sitting members of Congress for political purposes, specifically relating to the Joint Comprehensive Plan of Action (JCPOA) that was being negotiated at the time this information was collected," DeSantis wrote.[118]

---

118   http://freebeacon.com/national-security/
congress-seeks-investigation-into-obama-spy-ops-on-congress-israel/

Promoted a False Global Warming Narrative

In order to grab more power by setting the stage for more energy regulation, Obama has also openly lied about the "global warming," or "climate change" issue. Experts agree this is the case.

President Obama's statements on global warming are "dead wrong," said Nobel laureate Ivar Giaever, who rejected the president's claims that man-made global warming is causing climate change.

"I think Obama is a clever person, but he gets bad advice. Global warming is all wet," Giaever said in a speech entitled Global Warming Revisited he gave on July 1, 2015 to scientists from 90 countries attending the 65th annual Nobel Laureate Meeting in Lindau, Germany.

Giaever, who was born in Norway and became a naturalized U.S. citizen in 1964, was one of three recipients of the Nobel Prize for Physics in 1973.

"So global warming really starts with these two people: Al Gore and [former United Nations climate head Rajendra Pachauri," Giaever continued. "And what they did—they made this curve popular … And what did this curve measure? Well, this curve measures what is the average temperature for the world for a whole year … For one year. So there's an average temperature for the whole Earth for one year and that measures in a fraction of a degree."

"So what does that mean? I think probably nothing. Let me talk about that again: From 1880 to 2015, the temperature has increased from 288 K [degrees Kelvin] to 288.8 K—0.3 percent. I think the temperature has been amazingly stable.

"If I take where I live in Albany, New York, there is roughly an 80 K difference between summer and winter at some time, so would you think that a 0.8 degree average on the Earth makes any difference to the climate in Albany? Is that sensible to you?...

"I would say that global warming basically is a non-problem. Just leave it alone, it will take care of itself," he added.[119]

Other fascinating experts, including a cofounder of the Weather Channel, weigh in on the false climate change agenda:

On the same day that the U.N. Intergovernmental Panel on Climate Change issued a major new global warming report, John Coleman, a founder of the Weather Channel, appeared on CNN Sunday to reiterate his stance that "climate change is not happening."

Describing himself as a "skeptic," not a denier— "that is a word meant to put me down"—the veteran weather forecaster told CNN's "Reliable Sources" that the news network was promoting an inaccurate view on the issue.

"CNN has taken a very strong position on global warming, that it is a consensus," he said. "Well, there is no consensus in science. Science isn't a vote, science is about facts."[120]

119   http://cnsnews.com/news/article/kathleen-brown/
nobel-prize-winning-physicist-obama-dead-wrong-global-warming-0
120   http://cnsnews.com/news/article/patrick-goodenough/
weather-channel-founder-man-made-global-warming-baloney

Olympian Efforts to Change America

The images of a young, athletic Bruce Jenner are not hard to recall. After all, millions of boxes of Wheaties depicted the six-foot-two Olympic decathlon champion (in the 1976 games at Montreal) as the very picture of manliness.

Jenner went through a succession of marriages to beautiful women and amassed a fortune estimated at $100 million. The New York native remained youthful.

But as his celebrity grew late in his career due to his association with the Kardashian/reality show family, Jenner's long-time private life came to the surface.

He announced that he was making the physical transformation from the man the public knew to a woman he called "Caitlyn."

The effect on the public's consciousness was incredible. Equally confusing was his televised interview with Diane Sawyer where he said that he in fact wasn't gay but had in fact struggled all this life with the feeling that he was a woman trapped in a man's body.

What two generations ago would have been unthinkable then happened: America accepted and celebrated "Caitlyn."

Very soon after Jenner dropped his bombshell, the issue of "transgender bathrooms" surfaced. This Bizarro World introduction of a topic that almost defies description is simply the logical outcome of a society that has incrementally turned its back on God and His Word.

Think about this: we now live in a society when a man can claim to be a woman and then demand the use of the ladies' room in a restaurant or other public place. This literally exposes our children to the most grotesque forms of predatory behavior … yet our political and religious leaders do not come to the front and stand for traditional values.

CNN reported that Phil Robertson of Duck Dynasty fame "got a radical idea" on how to deal with the controversial transgender bathroom bill in North Carolina.

"Men should use the men's bathroom and women should use the women's bathroom," Robertson reportedly recently wrote. "Just because a man may 'feel' like a woman doesn't mean he should be able to share a bathroom with my daughter, or yours. That used to be called common sense. Now it's called bigoted."121

The fact that CNN called Robertson's statement "a radical idea" is a perfect example of how far off the country has become.

The perfect scripture to reflect these times is Isaiah 5:20: "Woe unto them that call evil good, and good evil; that put darkness for light, and light for darkness; that put bitter for sweet, and sweet for bitter!"

There are only a few nationally known evangelical leaders decrying this kind of madness. We've already documented the gradual evolution of our political leaders on these issues.

Democrat leaders are now emboldened. Napp Nazworth, a political analyst for the Christian Post, put it this way:

> Liberals are now totally fed up with deliberative democracy. The message is clear: "Obey, or you will be punished."
>
> On Friday, May 13, 2015, President Barack Obama directed all public schools in the country to base their bathroom and locker room usage rules on gender identity rather than sex. On an issue as sensitive as where we shower, change clothes and go potty, Obama decided there was no need for a public debate on the issue. No input from school boards, teachers, principles,

121   http://www.cnn.com/2016/05/10/entertainment/
phil-robertson-duck-dynasty-transgender/

superintendents, state legislatures, Congress or parents was required. Obama ruled for the nation.

This was not a one-off episode. For years now, Obama and his liberal cohorts have indicated they have no patience for deliberative democracy, in which issues are debated and compromises reached. Rather, they prefer to use court and executive actions to force their agenda on the rest of the nation.[122]

A whistleblower in the LGBT community has put forth the real motive:

What you may have been suspecting has been confirmed. LGBT activists' end goal is not ruling over the bathroom. It's obliterating the family. Riki Wilchins, a famous transsexual who recently wrote a piece in the gay publication The Advocate, revealed that many conservatives and even LGBT activists are missing the forest for the trees.

Titled, "We'll Win the Bathroom Battle When the Binary Burns," Wilchins says the real goal is to kill the notion of male and female altogether. The "binary" refers to gender distinction, and getting rid of the "heterobinary structure" is the goal. Wilchins writes that the fact that we are arguing over male and female facilities is proof that we still have far to go--that there should be no gender distinctions in general.

In fact, Wilchins points to an emerging group of people who don't want to affiliate as any gender. Life Site News explains, "'Non-binary' people don't identify as male or female and they often want to be referred

---

122   http://www.christianpost.com/news/
obama-doesnt-care-what-you-think-obey-or-you-will-be-punished-163870/

to as 'they' or 'hir' or 'zer.' So the fact that there are even intimate facilities that reflect the 'binary' truth about gender should change," Wilchins wrote.

If you are confused, you are not alone. But beneath all of the titles and non-titles, the insidious plan is the destruction of the family, reveals Stella Morabito, senior contributor to The Federalist.

"What we are really talking about is the abolition of sex. And it is sex that the trans project is serving to abolish legally, under the guise of something called 'the gender binary.' Its endgame is a society in which everyone is legally de-sexed. No longer legally male or female. And once you basically redefine humanity as sexless you end up with a de-humanized society in which there can be no legal 'mother' or 'father' or 'son' or 'daughter' or 'husband' or 'wife' without permission from the State. Government documents are already erasing the terms. In such a society, the most intimate human relationships take a hit. The family ends up abolished.

Morabito hits home the point: "Sex distinctions are the germ of all human relationships. Abolishing them legally basically abolishes family autonomy. And this is an act of violence against children because it would serve at some point to separate them from their origins. Every child's first transcendental question is 'Where did I come from?' If the law will not allow the child to see his own origins and wholeness in the faces of a mother and a father, it destabilizes the child's sense of self. It creates personal dysfunction in children and basically ends up spreading more dysfunction and even dystopia in society."

This is scary. If Morabito and other cultural watch-dogs are right, the bathroom battle is far more serious than many think. We need to really pray and ask God for help—before it's too late and our future generations end up really damaged. Do you agree?[123]

The Eroding Culture

The rise of social media has catapulted America over the edge of morality and common decency. I well remember the first time I was browsing a store's shelves and came across the now ubiquitous "selfie stick."

This simple device, a sort of short pole with a mount for a cellphone, allows the user to take "selfies" on his or her camera—surely this is the height of narcissistic behavior in American culture. There are current-ly 4.5 billion camera cellphones in the world, and the vast majority of them are used to transmit "selfies" to Facebook, Instagram, and Twitter. For what purpose?

So people can see us. We can gain attention.

This puts the lie to the long-held belief that humans simply suffer from a lack of self-esteem. In fact, as the prophecy teacher Arno Froese has said, his experience in counseling people over the years is that we have *too much* self-esteem, not a lack of it!

In truth, it is as the apostle Paul said, "After all, no one ever hated their own body, but they feed and care for their body" (Ephesians 5:29). America has become a self-absorbed collective of people adoring themselves.

---

123 http://www.faithfamilyamerica.com/famous_lgbt_activist_reveals_the_scary_real_goal_of_the_bathroom_battle_and_it_s_not_bathrooms_it_s_way_worse

This coarsening of the culture is seen in other ways, too.

Rock stars like Bruce Springsteen and Rogers Waters now refuse to perform in states that refuse to change their "bathroom rules" or in a country like Israel that stands up for our shared security values. Increasingly, the culture is seeking out music and film artists for their warped worldviews.

The actor Leonardo DiCaprio issues inane declarations about "climate change" while accepting an Oscar.

Kanye West begs for money to rescue him from losing a fortune.

"Comedian" Kathy Griffin utters the vilest statements about Christianity.

No one says a thing.

Conclusion

Make no mistake: Obama well knows that the (im)moral tone he has set for American youth has corroded the culture to such a point that we may have passed the point of no return. The unfortunate and sad situation is that once you lose turf, you don't win it back.

SO HELP ME GOD

CHAPTER 8

Woe unto them that call evil good, and good evil; that put darkness for light, and light for darkness; that put bitter for sweet, and sweet for bitter!

(Isaiah 5:20)

The Oath

The US Constitution specifies the exact language to be used in the oath given to an American President at their inauguration:

I do solemnly swear (or affirm) that I will faithfully execute the Office of president of the United States, and will to the best of my ability, preserve, protect and defend the Constitution of the United States.

According to numerous reports, President Barack Obama requested that at the end of the oath, the words "so help me God" be added.

The Library of Congress says those words were added by George Washington during the nation's first inauguration. Not all presidents have chosen to recite those words. A Bible is traditionally used in administering the oath.

Obama took the official oath on Sunday, January 20, 2013, at the White House with his left hand on the family Bible of his wife, Michelle.

At the Monday, January 21, 2013, ceremonial swearing-in at the Capitol, he used Bibles from Abraham Lincoln and Martin Luther King Jr.

When he said, "So help me God," what is he saying? Is he serious, or is this for public consumption?

The following would be appropriate for President Obama to make.

Promotion of Immorality

So help me God to understand that you know every thought I have, my motives, every plan I scheme and when I sin.

So help me God remember the scripture, "As I live, saith the Lord, every knee shall bow to me, and every tongue shall confess to God."[124]

So help me God understand the scripture, "Know ye not that the unrighteous shall not inherit the kingdom of God? Be not deceived: neither fornicators, nor idolaters, nor adulterers, nor effeminate, nor abusers of themselves with mankind."[125]

Promotion of False Religion

So help me God to understand that my telling people that there are other paths to God is blasphemy and false according to the Bible.

---

124   Romans 14:11
125   1 Corinthians 6:9–10

So help me God know that bowing to or honoring other religions that are in direct opposition to the Bible is blasphemy.

So help me God rid me from the damage from have attended a hate-filled anti-Semitic church for twenty years.

So help me God for my wrongfully stating and not understanding people's concerns, "When I hear folks say that, well, maybe we should just admit the Christians but not the Muslims [into the U.S.], when I hear political leaders suggesting that there would be a religious test for which person who's fleeing from a war-torn country is admitted … that's shameful."[126]

So help me God for wrongfully stating in a visit to India, "In our lives, Michelle and I have been strengthened by our Christian faith. But there have been times where my faith has been questioned—by people who don't know me—or they've said that I adhere to a different religion, as if that were somehow a bad thing."[127]

So help me God for wrongfully saying at the National Prayer Breakfast, "And lest we get on our high horse and think this is unique to some other place, remember that during the Crusades and the Inquisition, people committed terrible deeds in the name of Christ. In our home country, slavery and Jim Crow all too often was justified in the name of Christ. Michelle and I returned from India—an incredible, beautiful country, full of magnificent diversity—but a place where, in past years, religious faiths of all types have, on occasion, been targeted by other peoples of faith, simply due to their heritage and their beliefs—acts of

---

126   Obama: It's "Shameful" to "Say We Should Just Admit the Christians But Not the Muslims," http://www.cnsnews.com/news/article/melanie-hunter/ obama-shameful-suggest-there-would-be-religious-test-people-fleeing
127   Remarks by President Obama in Address to the People of India, https://www.whitehouse.gov/the-press-office/2015/01/27/ remarks-president-obama-address-people-india

intolerance that would have shocked Gandhi, the person who helped to liberate that nation."[128]

So help me God to understand that it was inappropriate for me to opine the following at an Easter Prayer Breakfast at the White House, "On Easter, I do reflect on the fact that as a Christian, I am supposed to love," Mr. Obama said toward the end of his speech. "And I have to say that sometimes when I listen to less-than-loving expressions by Christians, I get concerned."[129]

So help me God know when I stated, "Where there is injustice we defend the oppressed, where there is disagreement, we treat each other with compassion and respect. Where there are differences, we find strength in our common humanity, knowing that we are all children of God" is not accurate. All people are created by God, but the children of God are those who have received Jesus as their Savior, not Buddhists, Muslims, Hindus, atheists, and agnostics.[130]

So help me God understand that I and my administration were wrong for inviting a pro-abortion nun, the first openly gay Episcopal bishop, at least two openly gay Catholic activists, and a biological woman who identifies as a man to be among the thousand that greeted Pope Francis at the White House in September 2015. It was outrageous and insulting.[131]

So help me God know that inviting gay bishops, lesbian reverends, and religious leaders that approve of same-sex marriage to Easter prayer breakfasts is an abomination to God.

---

128   Remarks by the President at National Prayer Breakfast, https://www.whitehouse.gov/the-press-office/2015/02/05/remarks-president-national-prayer-breakfast
129   Remarks by the President and the Vice President at Easter Prayer Breakfast, https://www.whitehouse.gov/the-press-office/2015/04/07/remarks-president-and-vice-president-easter-prayer-breakfast
130   Ibid.
131   For Pope's visit, Obama invites a pro-abort nun, gay Episcopal bishop, and LGBT "Catholic" activists, https://www.lifesitenews.com/news/for-popes-visit-obama-invites-a-pro-abort-nun-gay-episcopal-bishop-and-lgbt

Speech to the Muslim World—Cairo, Egypt—June 4, 2009

So help me God to understand that my speech to the Muslim world from Cairo, Egypt, on June 4, 2009, was filled with distortions and inaccuracies that greatly confused people and endangered America.

So help me God to quit speaking as if Allah is the same as the God of the Bible. Allah is not.

So help me God to understand the confusion I have created for honoring Islam, a religion that is in direct opposition to Christianity.

So help me God understand that my confusing comments to the Muslim world about the copy of the Koran in Thomas Jefferson's library was not to honor it—and that the real reason was to better understand the Muslim Barbary pirates who were hijacking merchant ships.

So help me God for falsely comparing the horrific Jewish Holocaust to the plight of the Palestinians, who have been robbed by their corrupt leaders.

So help me God to stop distorting American history by stating Muslims had a significant role in making America great.

Islam

So help me God to understand that Islam is not a religion of peace and the Koran is not a book of peace.

So help me God understand that spending many hours defending Islam while spending almost zero time speaking of the horrible persecution of Christians in the Middle East by radical Muslims is unconscionable.

So help me God for not addressing or doing anything about the many Christians being persecuted in countries throughout the Middle East since the beginning of the Arab Spring in January 2011.

So help me God publicly admit the danger of providing access to the Muslim Brotherhood at top levels within my administration.[132]

So help me God to understand why American allies in the Middle East don't trust me, and enemies don't fear me.

So help me God that this statement on Muhammad at a Baltimore mosque is false, "Whoever wants to enter paradise, the Prophet Muhammad taught, 'let him treat people the way he would love to be treated,' is confusing, especially for my stating a Christians like myself.[133]

LGBT promotion

So help me God to understand that promoting a lesbian, gay, bisexual, and transgender agenda (LGBT) is an outrage to God in the Old and New Testaments.

So help me God to fully understand, "For the wrath of God is revealed from heaven against all ungodliness and unrighteousness of men, who hold the truth in unrighteousness."[134]

So help me God fully understand that God hates the sin.[135]

So help me God for wrongfully proclaiming that the Defense of Marriage Act (DOMA) was unconstitutional and for instructing my attorney general not to defend it. This led to seven state attorney generals to do the same.[136]

So help me God to repent for declaring that I have done more than forty-three previous US presidents to promote the homosexual and bisexual agenda.

---

132   General: Muslim Brotherhood Inside Obama Administration,
http://www.wnd.com/2014/01/general-muslim-brotherhood-inside-obama-administration/
133   Remarks by the President at Islamic Society of Baltimore,
http://www.wnd.com/2014/01/general-muslim-brotherhood-inside-obama-administration/
134   Romans 1:18
135   Ibid.
136   In Shift, U.S. Says Marriage Act Blocks Gay Rights, http://www.nytimes.com/2011/02/24/us/24marriage.html?pagewanted=all&_r=0

So help me God to understand I am responsible for promoting an immoral lifestyle in the United States and through the United Nations, and that I have wrongfully threatened to stop US aid to nations that don't support the LGBT movement.

So help me God to understand that as commander in chief, I should not have forced generals at the Pentagon to agree to my "don't ask, don't tell" agenda, contrary to their biblical beliefs, and that this has and will have consequences for our military, our nation, and me.

So help me God to understand that military chaplains have experienced persecution for their biblical beliefs, were forced out of the military for praying in Jesus Christ's name, or be obligated to perform same-sex marriages because of my forcing "Don't ask, don't tell" on the US military.

So help me God to understand that my using "love wins" after the Supreme Court's same-sex marriage decisions doesn't lessen the consequences of sin.

So help me God to understand equal rights is not an excuse for sinful behavior.

So help me God to understand my declaring same-sex marriage is marriage equality is an abomination.

So help me God understand that having a rainbow shine on the White House the day the Supreme Court voted in favor of same-sex marriage is an insult to God-fearing and God-honoring Christians.

So help me God understand this is revealing of my motives, "Former Defense Secretary Robert Gates sharply questions President Obama's 'passion' for military matters in his forthcoming memoir, and claims that practically the only time he saw that in the president was during his push to repeal 'Don't Ask, Don't Tell.'"[137]

137   Gates: "Don't ask, don't tell" fight was only time Obama showed "passion" for military issues, http://www.foxnews.com/politics/2014/01/12/gates-dont-ask-dont-tell-fight-was-only-time-obama-showed-passion-for-military.html

So help me God know that filling my administration with over 250 well-positioned LGBT activists is an affront to you. They are in key positions at Labor, Commerce, State Department, the Defense Department, the Supreme Court, Education, and most other branches of the federal government. Very few Americans realize the depth of this because 85 to 90 percent of the US media condones it, helps facilitate it, or doesn't write about it.[138]

So help me God to know that it is wrong for stating the following before a national Super Bowl audience on February 3, 2013, "My attitude is that gays and lesbians should have access and opportunities, the same way as everyone else does, in every institution and walk of life." He continued, "And you know the Scouts are a great institution, that are promoting young people and exposing them to opportunities and leadership that will serve people for the rest of their lives. And I think nobody should be barred from that."[139]

Damage to America

So help me God understand that by using executive orders and czars to circumvent the Constitution, I am not fulfilling the oath of office that I swore to uphold.

So help me God to understand it is wrong for me to initiate class warfare or ethnic division through speeches and policies.

So help me God to understand it is not godly to verbally attack people, distort their backgrounds, and malign their reputations in campaigns.

---

138   Building Successful LGBT Leaders,
https://www.victoryinstitute.org/programs/presidential-appointments
139   Obama Talks Football, Gender Issues, Taxes Before Super Bowl,
http://abcnews.go.com/blogs/politics/2013/02/
obama-talks-football-gender-issues-taxes-before-super-bowl/

So help me God to understand that the fact the US federal debt will climb to $20 trillion during my time in office is irresponsible and bankrupting the United States.[140]

So help me God to fully understand that you are Sovereign over our climate and everything that happens on earth and that it is pure arrogance to think that humanity controls the climate cycles when it occupies only a small part of the planet and two-thirds of earth is covered by water.

Abortion and Contraceptives

So help me God to understand that you knew us before we were formed in our mothers' wombs, and that I should personally stop supporting the slaughter of preborn children in their mothers' wombs.

So help me God to understand that there is no greater violence known to man than the ripping apart of a preborn child in her mother's womb, which has happened 56 million times since 1973.

So help me God to stop supporting the annual financial support for Planned Parenthood, which boasted of performing 330,000 abortions of preborn children in their mothers' wombs in 2012.

So help me God to stop my administration from forcing Christian organizations or any others that refuse to offer their employees access to the morning-after and week-after pill intended to prevent pregnancy after known or suspected contraceptive failure or unprotected sex.[141]

140    $20 trillion man: National debt nearly doubles during Obama presidency, http://www.washingtontimes.com/news/2015/nov/1/ obama-presidency-to-end-with-20-trillion-national-/?page=all
141   Hobby Lobby to Supreme Court: Protect Us From $1.3M in Fines a Day Over Obamacare, http://www.lifenews.com/2014/02/10/ hobby-lobby-to-supreme-court-protect-us-from-1-3m-in-fines-a-day-over-obamacare/

Israel

So help me God to understand that I must stop pressuring Israel to accept an Arab state in the Promised Land of Judea, Samaria, and East Jerusalem—land that was given by God to Abraham, Isaac, Jacob, and their descendants in an everlasting and unconditional covenant.

So help me God to stop pressuring Israel to divide land that would give them indefensible borders and endanger their future.

So help me God to understand that my Middle East policies, my promotion of the Arab Spring, my relationship with the Muslim Brotherhood, and lack of involvement against radical Islamists are endangering the region and leaving Israel in great danger on its borders and internally.

So help me God understand that the Iran nuclear deal that I initiated endangers Israel, the Middle East countries that border the Persian Gulf, and world economies if oil delivery is disrupted, and that the release of $100 billion to the number one state sponsor of terror in the world is insanity. The leadership of Iran continues to call the United States the Great Satan and Israel the Little Satan.

Finally

It is hard to fully comprehend and extrapolate the extent of present and long-term damage that has occurred and will after the eight years Barack Obama has been President of the United States.

No US administration has done more to accelerate the nation toward biblical judgment than Obama's. History shows that God is long suffering, but eventual judgment of the leaders, nations, and the institutions will be sudden and swift unless there is repentance.

We pray that these previous "So Help Me God" statements will move the President to personal repentance and call for the nation to repent.

If my people, who are called by my name, will humble themselves and pray and seek my face and turn from their wicked ways, then I will hear from heaven, and I will forgive their sin and will heal their land.

(2 Chronicles 7:14)

APPENDIX 1:
Obama's Opening Statement at Al-Azhar—a Muslim University

(With commentary and analysis by Bill Koenig)

[Note: President Obama's remarks are italicized]

PRESIDENT OBAMA: Thank you very much. Good afternoon. I am honored to be in the timeless city of Cairo and to be hosted by two remarkable institutions. For over a thousand years, Al-Azhar has stood as a beacon of Islamic learning; and for over a century, Cairo University has been a source of Egypt's advancement. And together, you represent the harmony between tradition and progress.

I'm grateful for your hospitality, and the hospitality of the people of Egypt. And I'm also proud to carry with me the goodwill of the American people, and a greeting of peace from Muslim communities in my country: Assalaamu alaykum. (Applause)

Note from Wikipedia: The speech was given at Al-Azhar University in Egypt, which was founded in 975 and is the chief center of Arabic literature and Sunni Islamic learning in the world. It also is the world's second-oldest surviving degree-granting university. It is associated with Al-Azhar mosque in Islamic Cairo. The university's mission includes the propagation of Islamic religion and culture. To this end, its Islamic scholars (ulemas) render edicts (fatwas) on disputes submitted to them from all over the Sunni Islamic world regarding proper conduct for Muslim individuals or societies. Al-Azhar also trains Egyptian government–appointed preachers in proselytization (da'wa).

Al-Azhar is to launch Islamic TV channel dedicated to giving "the world a better understanding of Islam"

Egypt's seat of Islamic learning, Al Azhar, will launch a satellite channel to give the world a better understanding of Islam and to counter some Islamic outlets preaching "extremist dialogue," its architects said yesterday.

Sheikh Khaled al-Guindy, a scholar at Al Azhar mosque and university, said the new channel will reach out to the world's 1.5 billion Muslims and non-Muslims alike.

"In the Age of Obama we realized it was time to look at new ways to deliver our message," Guindy said, four days before US President Barack Obama visited Egypt to address the Muslim world. The launch is planned for the start of Ramadan in mid-August.

Koenig: This announcement was given on May 31, a few days before Obama's speech. In other words, Obama's speech helped launch the new Arab TV network.

Obama has called for new beginning between the United States and Muslims:

I've come here to Cairo to seek a new beginning between the United States and Muslims around the world, one based on mutual interest and mutual respect, and one based upon the truth that America and Islam are not exclusive and need not be in competition. Instead, they overlap and share common principles—principles of justice and progress, tolerance and the dignity of all human beings.

Koenig: This overlap of principles is a complete distortion—pure rhetoric.

Obama spoke of moving forward, while quoting the Koran:

But I am convinced that in order to move forward, we must say openly to each other the things we hold in our hearts and that too often are said only behind closed doors. There must be a sustained effort to listen to each other; to learn from each other; to respect one another; and to seek common ground. As the Holy Koran tells us, "Be conscious of God and speak always the truth." (Applause)

That is what I will try to do today—to speak the truth as best I can, humbled by the task before us, and firm in my belief that the interests we share as human beings are far more powerful than the forces that drive us apart.

Koenig: A plug for the Koran.

Obama's Muslim experience:

Now, part of this conviction is rooted in my own experience. I'm a Christian, but my father came from a Kenyan family that includes generations of Muslims. As a boy, I spent several years in Indonesia and heard the call of the azaan at the break of dawn and at the fall of dusk. As a young man, I worked in Chicago communities where many found dignity and peace in their Muslim faith.

As a student of history, I also know civilization's debt to Islam. It was Islam—at places like Al-Azhar—that carried the light of learning through so many centuries, paving the way for Europe's Renaissance and Enlightenment.

It was innovation in Muslim communities—(applause)—it was innovation in Muslim communities that developed the order of algebra; our

magnetic compass and tools of navigation; our mastery of pens and print-
ing; our understanding of how disease spreads and how it can be healed.

Islamic culture has given us majestic arches and soaring spires; time-
less poetry and cherished music; elegant calligraphy and places of peaceful
contemplation.

And throughout history, Islam has demonstrated through words and
deeds the possibilities of religious tolerance and racial equality. (Applause)

Koenig: Obama distorted history in order to engage his audience.

Obama on Islam as part of America's story:

I also know that Islam has always been a part of America's story. The
first nation to recognize my country was Morocco. In signing the Treaty
of Tripoli in 1796, our second president, John Adams, wrote, "The United
States has in itself no character of enmity against the laws, religion or tran-
quility of Muslims."

And since our founding, American Muslims have enriched the United
States. They have fought in our wars, they have served in our government,
they have stood for civil rights, they have started businesses, they have
taught at our universities, they've excelled in our sports arenas, they've won
Nobel Prizes, built our tallest building, and lit the Olympic Torch.

And when the first Muslim American was recently elected to Congress,
he took the oath to defend our Constitution using the same Holy Koran that
one of our Founding Fathers—Thomas Jefferson—kept in his personal li-
brary. (Applause)

Koenig: He should have given some names and specifics. Once
again, he delivered more distortions.

From the article, "Thomas Jefferson, Ben Franklin, John Adams
and James Madison: Young America's Fight with Islamism," by Andrew
Walden:

In light of the reference to the 1796 "Treaty of Tripoli" in Obama's Cairo speech:

Obama stated: "In signing the Treaty of Tripoli in 1796, our second President John Adams wrote, 'The United States has in itself no character of enmity against the laws, religion or tranquility of Muslims.'" (Obama took the words out of context; they are underlined .)

Articles 10 and 11 from the 1796 "Treaty of Tripoli":

Art. 10. The money and presents demanded by the Dey of Tripoli, as a full and satisfactory consideration on his part, and on the part of his subjects, for this treaty of perpetual peace and friendship, are acknowledged to have been received by him previous to his signing the same, according to a receipt which is hereto annexed, except such as part as is promised, on the part of the United States, to be delivered and paid by them on the arrival of their Consul in Tripoli; of which part a note is likewise hereto annexed. And no pretense of any periodical tribute of further payments is ever to be made by either party.

Art. 11. As the Government of the United States of America is not, in any sense, founded on the Christian religion; as it has in itself no character of enmity against the laws, religion, or tranquility, of Mussulmen [Muslims]; and, as the said States never entered into any war, or act of hostility against any Mahometan nation, it is declared by the parties, that no pretext arising from religious opinions, shall ever produce an interruption of the harmony existing between the two countries. (Section read by Obama in italics. Sections violated by Barbary States underlined .)

Koenig: These articles in the treaty speak of ransom money paid to the Muslim pirates, and the appeasement statement is not the way Obama used the example. This is gross distortion and a bad reflection on the United States when the Muslims were the culprits and the thieves.

Andrew Walden further wrote:

> America has been fighting Islamists for longer than many people realize. Even before independence was declared, American ships were pirated, and their Christian crews enslaved, by Muslim pirates operating under the control of "Dey of Algiers"—an Ottoman Islamist warlord ruling Algeria.
>
> When the colonists rebelled against British rule in 1776, American ships lost Royal Navy protection. A Revolutionary War-era alliance with France offered French protection to U.S. ships, but it expired in 1783. Immediately, U.S. ships came under attack; and in October 1784, the American trader "Betsey" was taken by Moroccan forces. This was followed with Algerians and Libyans (Tripolitans) capturing two more U.S. ships in 1785.
>
> Lacking the ability to project U.S. naval force in the Mediterranean, America tried appeasement. In 1784, Congress agreed to fund tributes and ransoms in order to rescue U.S. ships and buy the freedom of enslaved American sailors.
>
> In 1786, Thomas Jefferson, then U.S. ambassador to France, and John Adams, then American ambassador to Britain, met in London with Sidi Haji Abdul Rahman Adja, the Dey's ambassador to Britain, in an attempt to negotiate a peace treaty based on Congress' vote of

funding. To Congress, these two future presidents later reported the reasons for the Muslims' hostility towards America, a nation with which they had no previous contacts.

"... that it was founded on the Laws of their Prophet, that it was written in their Koran, that all nations who should not have acknowledged their authority were sinners, that it was their right and duty to make war upon them wherever they could be found, and to make slaves of all they could take as Prisoners, and that every Musselman (Muslim) who should be slain in Battle was sure to go to Paradise."

By 1800, the annual tribute and ransom payments first agreed in the mid-1780s (and supposedly ended under the 1796 Treaty of Tripoli) amounted to about $1 million—20 percent of the federal budget. (For fiscal year 2007, 20 percent of US revenues would equal $560 billion.)

In May, 1801, Yussif Karamanli, the Pasha of Tripoli, declared war on America by chopping down the flagpole in front of the US Consulate. Seventeen years after appeasement and tribute payments had begun, President Thomas Jefferson led America into the First Barbary War.

Note: John Quincy Adams, "Christianity—Islamism: Unsigned essays dealing with the Russo-Turkish War, and on Greece," originally published in *The American Annual Register for 1827–1829* (New York, 1830), Chs. X–XIV: 267–402.

You would think that the evidence of knowledge from the past would mean that Islam was a known enemy, but it has not been taught so. Thomas Jefferson fought wars with Muslim pirates who lived by the Koran. That is why he kept a copy of it. The wars he fought were called the Barbary Wars, from 1801 to 1805. They were to free Americans taken as slaves from American merchant ships.

The government spent millions of dollars to get them back at a time when private citizens were financing much of the government from their own pockets, with little or no reimbursements! *And* it was the first time a president (Jefferson) initiated a war without Congress's approval, so it was very controversial. He did it while they were adjourned. But the Americans were freed in the end. Jefferson knew from 1801 to 1805, and Adams knew in 1827, the same thing!

Obama on a partnership with Islam:

"So I have known Islam on three continents before coming to the region where it was first revealed. That experience guides my conviction that partnership between America and Islam must be based on what Islam is, not what it isn't. And I consider it part of my responsibility as president of the United States to fight against negative stereotypes of Islam wherever they appear." (Applause)

Koenig: What is Islam? Look at the Koran, which guides this religion—and look at its history of relationships not only with others but with various internal factions. Why should the president of the United States be responsible to fight against negative stereotypes of Islam wherever they appear?

Obama on his name, Barack Hussein Obama:

"Now, much has been made of the fact that an African American with the name Barack Hussein Obama could be elected president. (Applause) But my personal story is not so unique. The dream of opportunity for all people has not come true for everyone in America, but its promise exists for all who come to our shores—and that includes nearly 7 million American Muslims in our country today who, by the way, enjoy incomes and educational levels that are higher than the American average. (Applause)

Moreover, freedom in America is indivisible from the freedom to prac-
tice one's religion. That is why there is a mosque in every state in our union
and over 1,200 mosques within our borders. That's why the United States
government has gone to court to protect the right of women and girls to
wear the hijab and to punish those who would deny it. (Applause)

Koenig: Obama never uses Hussein in the United States, but he does
when he speaks to Muslim audiences.

Also, 7 million US Muslims is a gross exaggeration. Daniel Pipes
wrote: "A good round estimate is that Muslims make up just under 1 percent of the U.S. population or in the neighborhood of 3 million people"
(April 22, 2003).

Obama said Islam is a part of America:

"So let there be no doubt: Islam is a part of America. And I believe that
America holds within her the truth that regardless of race, religion, or sta-
tion in life, all of us share common aspirations—to live in peace and secu-
rity; to get an education and to work with dignity; to love our families, our
communities and our God."

Koenig: This is Obama's unofficial opening of the door of America
to a greater involvement of Islam. Can you imagine Adams, Jefferson,
Franklin, other founding fathers, or previous presidents stating that Islam is part of America?

Obama on the Koran:

And that's why we're partnering with a coalition of 46 countries. And
despite the costs involved, America's commitment will not weaken. Indeed,
none of us should tolerate these extremists. They have killed in many coun-
tries. They have killed people of different faiths—but more than any other,
they have killed Muslims. Their actions are irreconcilable with the rights
of human beings, the progress of nations, and with Islam. The Holy Koran

teaches that whoever kills an innocent is as—it is as if he has killed all mankind. (Applause)

And the Holy Koran also says whoever saves a person, it is as if he has saved all mankind. (Applause) The enduring faith of over a billion people is so much bigger than the narrow hatred of a few. Islam is not part of the problem in combating violent extremism—it is an important part of promoting peace.

Former President John Quincy Adams on the Koran

As Andrew Boston wrote in Front Page Magazine: John Quincy Adams possessed a remarkably clear, uncompromised understanding of the permanent Islamic institutions of jihad war and *dhimmitude*. Regarding jihad, Adams stated in his essay series: "… he [Muhammad] declared undistinguishing and exterminating war, as a part of his religion, against all the rest of mankind … The precept of the Koran is, perpetual war against all who deny, that Mahomet is the prophet of God."

APPENDIX 2:

OBAMA:
Muslim Apologist,
America's Top LGBT Activist,
Most Biblically-Hostile U. S.
President

[In his own words and boasts of accomplishments]

[Emphasis Added]

Muslim Apologist[1]

"We Do Not Consider Ourselves A Christian Nation"

https://www.youtube.com/watch?v=QIVd7YT0oWA

"Whatever we once were, we are no longer a Christian nation"

http://www.americanthinker.com/articles/2009/04/obamas_
christian_nation_1.html

"The future must not belong to those who slander the Prophet of Islam"

> http://www.faithstreet.com/onfaith/2012/09/26/obama-the-future-must-not-belong-to-those-who-slander-the-prophet-of-islam/11183

"The sweetest sound I know is the Muslim call to prayer"

> http://www.raptureready.com/featured/duck/dd74.html

"I also know that Islam has always been a part of America's story."

> https://www.whitehouse.gov/the-press-office/remarks-president-cairo-university-6-04-09

"I made clear that America is not – and never will be – at war with Islam."

> https://www.whitehouse.gov/the-press-office/remarks-president-cairo-university-6-04-09

"Islam has always been part of America"

> https://www.whitehouse.gov/the-press-office/remarks-president-cairo-university-6-04-09

"Islam has a proud tradition of tolerance."

> https://www.whitehouse.gov/the-press-office/remarks-president-cairo-university-6-04-09

"As a student of history, I also know civilization's debt to Islam."

> https://www.whitehouse.gov/the-press-office/
> remarks-president-cairo-university-6-04-09

"Throughout history, Islam has demonstrated through words and deeds the possibilities of religious tolerance and racial equality."

> https://www.whitehouse.gov/the-press-office/
> remarks-president-cairo-university-6-04-09

"We will encourage more Americans to study in Muslim communities"

> https://www.whitehouse.gov/the-press-office/
> remarks-president-cairo-university-6-04-09

Obama compares the plight of Middle Eastern refugees to the Pilgrims

> https://www.whitehouse.gov/the-press-office/2015/11/26/
> weekly-address-thanksgiving-recognizing-greatness-ameri-
> can-generosity

The White House

Office of the Press Secretary

For Immediate Release - November 25, 2015

Weekly Address: This Thanksgiving, Recognizing the Greatness of American Generosity

WASHINGTON, DC — In this week's address, the President wished everyone a happy Thanksgiving, and reflected on America's history of welcoming men and women seeking a safer, better future for themselves and their families. On this uniquely American holiday, he recognized the greatness of American generosity, as evidenced by people are the country who use the day to volunteer and give back to others. And he shared stories of Americans who, in that same spirit of generosity, have written letters to him expressing their willingness to open their homes to refugees fleeing the brutality of ISIL. Like the pilgrims who set sail on the Mayflower nearly four centuries ago, these refugees are looking for safety and another chance. And it is important to remember that they undergo the highest security checks of anyone traveling to the United States. The President reminded us that providing refuge to some of the world's most vulnerable people is an American tradition, and part of what makes this country the greatest on Earth.

Remarks of President Barack Obama Weekly Address The White House November 26, 2015

Hi, everybody. In 1620, a small band of pilgrims came to this continent, refugees who had fled persecution and violence in their native land. Nearly 400 years later, we remember their part in the American story — and we honor the men and women who helped them in their time of need.

Thanksgiving is a day for food and football, and for hoping the turkey didn't turn out too dry. But it's also a day to count our blessings and give back to others — a reminder that no matter our circumstances, all of us have something to be grateful for. Maybe it's good health, a new addition to the family, or a child taking a next step toward college or a career. Maybe it's a new job, or long overdue raise. Maybe it's something as simple, and as important, as the chance to spend time with the people who matter most.

Of course, every American can be thankful for the chance to live in a country founded on the belief that all of us are created equal. And as President, I'm thankful that I get to see the best of America every day — the courage of our troops and veterans, the resilience of our families, and the basic goodness of the ordinary people who call this country.

On this uniquely American holiday, we also remember that so much of our greatness comes from our generosity. There's the generosity of Americans who volunteer at food banks and shelters, making sure that no one goes hungry on a day when so many plates are full. There's the generosity of Americans who take part not just in Black Friday and Cyber Monday, but Giving Tuesday — recognizing that in the holiday season, what you give is as important as what you get.

And I've been touched by the generosity of the Americans who've written me letters and emails in recent weeks, offering to open their homes to refugees fleeing the brutality of ISIL.

Now, people should remember that no refugee can enter our borders until they undergo the highest security checks of anyone traveling to the United States. That was the case before Paris, and it's the case now. And what happened in Paris hasn't stopped Americans from opening their arms anyway.

One woman from Pennsylvania wrote me to say, "Money is tight for us in my household ... But i have a guest room. I have a pantry full of food. We can do this." Another woman from Florida told me her family's history dates back to the Mayflower — and she said that welcoming others is part of "what it means to be an American."

Nearly four centuries after the Mayflower set sail, the world is still full of pilgrims — men and women who want nothing more than the chance for a safer, better future for themselves and their families. What makes America America is that we offer that chance. We turn Lady Liberty's light to the world, and widen our circle of concern to say that all God's children are worthy of our compassion and care. That's part of what makes this the greatest country on Earth.

I hope that you and your family have wonderful Thanksgiving, surrounded by loved ones, and full of joy and gratitude. And together, may we all play our own small part in the American story, and write a next chapter that future generations can be thankful for.

From the Obama family to yours, have a great Thanksgiving.

Obama's major speech on Islam in America

https://www.whitehouse.gov/the-press-office/2016/02/03/remarks-president-islamic-society-baltimore

The White House

Office of the Press Secretary

For Immediate Release - February 03, 2016

Remarks by the President at Islamic Society of Baltimore

Baltimore, Maryland

1:04 P.M. EST

THE PRESIDENT: Well, good afternoon. And, Sabah, thank you for the wonderful introduction and for your example — your devotion to your faith and your education, and your service to others. You're an inspiration. You're going to be a fantastic doctor. And I suspect, Sabah, your parents are here because they wanted to see you so — where are

Sabah's parents? There you go. (Applause.) Good job, Mom. She did great, didn't she? She was terrific.

To everyone here at the Islamic Society of Baltimore, thank you for welcoming me here today. I want to thank Muslim Americans leaders from across this city and this state, and some who traveled even from out of state to be here. I want to recognize Congressman John Sarbanes, who is here. (Applause.) As well as two other great leaders in Congress — and proud Muslim Americans — Congressman Keith Ellison from the great state of Minnesota — (applause) — and Congressman Andre Carson from the great state of Indiana. (Applause.)

This mosque, like so many in our country, is an all-American story. You've been part of this city for nearly half a century. You serve thousands of families — some who've lived here for decades as well as immigrants from many countries who've worked to become proud American citizens.

Now, a lot of Americans have never visited a mosque. To the folks watching this today who haven't — think of your own church, or synagogue, or temple, and a mosque like this will be very familiar. This is where families come to worship and express their love for God and each other. There's a school where teachers open young minds. Kids play baseball and football and basketball — boys and girls — I hear they're pretty good. (Laughter.) Cub Scouts, Girl Scouts meet, recite the Pledge of Allegiance here.

With interfaith dialogue, you build bridges of understanding with other faith communities — Christians and Jews. There's a health clinic that serves the needy, regardless of their faith. And members of this community are out in the broader community, working for social justice and urban development. As voters, you come here to meet candidates. As one of your members said, "just look at the way we live...we are true Americans."

So the first thing I want to say is two words that Muslim Americans don't hear often enough — and that is, thank you. Thank you for serving your community. Thank you for lifting up the lives of your neighbors, and for helping keep us strong and united as one American family. We are grateful for that. (Applause.)

Now, this brings me to the other reason I wanted to come here today. I know that in Muslim communities across our country, this is a time of concern and, frankly, a time of some fear. Like all Americans, you're worried about the threat of terrorism. But on top of that, as Muslim Americans, you also have another concern — and that is your entire community so often is targeted or blamed for the violent acts of the very few.

The Muslim American community remains relatively small —several million people in this country. And as a result, most Americans don't necessarily know — or at least don't know that they know — a Muslim personally. And as a result, many only hear about Muslims and Islam from the news after an act of terrorism, or in distorted media portrayals in TV or film, all of which gives this hugely distorted impression.

And since 9/11, but more recently, since the attacks in Paris and San Bernardino, you've seen too often people conflating the horrific acts of terrorism with the beliefs of an entire faith. And of course, recently, we've heard inexcusable political rhetoric against Muslim Americans that has no place in our country.

No surprise, then, that threats and harassment of Muslim Americans have surged. Here at this mosque, twice last year, threats were made against your children. Around the country, women wearing the hijab — just like Sabah — have been targeted.

We've seen children bullied. We've seen mosques vandalized. Sikh Americans and others who are perceived to be Muslims have been targeted, as well.

I just had a chance to meet with some extraordinary Muslim Americans from across the country who are doing all sorts of work. Some of them are doctors; some of them are community leaders; religious leaders. All of them were doing extraordinary work not just in the Muslim community but in the American community. And they're proud of their work in business and education, and on behalf of social justice and the environment and education. I should point out they were all much younger than me — (laughter) — which is happening more frequently these days. And you couldn't help but be inspired, hearing about the extraordinary work that they're doing. But you also could not help but be heartbroken to hear their worries and their anxieties.

Some of them are parents, and they talked about how their children were asking, are we going to be forced out of the country, or, are we going to be rounded up? Why do people treat us like that? Conversations that you shouldn't have to have with children — not in this country. Not at this moment.

And that's an anxiety echoed in letters I get from Muslim Americans around the country. I've had people write to me and say, I feel like I'm a second-class citizen. I've had mothers write and say, "my heart cries every night," thinking about how her daughter might be treated at school. A girl from Ohio, 13 years old, told me, "I'm scared." A girl from Texas signed her letter "a confused 14-year-old trying to find her place in the world."

These are children just like mine. And the notion that they would be filled with doubt and questioning their places in this great country of ours at a time when they've got enough to worry about — it's hard being a teenager already — that's not who we are.

We're one American family. And when any part of our family starts to feel separate or second-class or targeted, it tears at the very fabric of our nation. (Applause.)

It's a challenge to our values — and that means we have much work to do. We've got to tackle this head on. We have to be honest and clear about it. And we have to speak out. This is a moment when, as Americans, we have to truly listen to each other and learn from each other. And I believe it has to begin with a common understanding of some basic facts. And I express these facts, although they'd be obvious to many of the people in this place, because, unfortunately, it's not facts that are communicated on a regular basis through our media.

So let's start with this fact: For more than a thousand years, people have been drawn to Islam's message of peace. And the very word itself, Islam, comes from salam — peace. The standard greeting is as-salamu alaykum — peace be upon you. And like so many faiths, Islam is rooted in a commitment to compassion and mercy and justice and charity. Whoever wants to enter paradise, the Prophet Muhammad taught, "let him treat people the way he would love to be treated." (Applause.) For Christians like myself, I'm assuming that sounds familiar. (Laughter.)

The world's 1.6 billion Muslims are as diverse as humanity itself. They are Arabs and Africans. They're from Latin America to Southeast Asia; Brazilians, Nigerians, Bangladeshis, Indonesians. They are white and brown and black. There's a large African American Muslim community. That diversity is represented here today. A 14-year-old boy in Texas who's Muslim spoke for many when he wrote to me and said, "We just want to live in peace."

Here's another fact: Islam has always been part of America. Starting in colonial times, many of the slaves brought here from Africa were Muslim. And even in their bondage, some kept their faith alive. A few even won their freedom and became known to many Americans. And when enshrining the freedom of religion in our Constitution and our Bill of Rights, our Founders meant what they said when they said it applied to all religions.

Back then, Muslims were often called Mahometans. And Thomas Jefferson explained that the Virginia Statute for Religious Freedom he wrote was designed to protect all faiths — and I'm quoting Thomas Jefferson now — "the Jew and the Gentile, the Christian and the Mahometan." (Applause.)

Jefferson and John Adams had their own copies of the Koran. Benjamin Franklin wrote that "even if the Mufti of Constantinople were to send a missionary to preach to us, he would find a pulpit at his service." (Applause.) So this is not a new thing.

Generations of Muslim Americans helped to build our nation. They were part of the flow of immigrants who became farmers and merchants. They built America's first mosque, surprisingly enough, in North Dakota. (Laughter.) America's oldest surviving mosque is in Iowa. The first Islamic center in New York City was built in the 1890s. Muslim Americans worked on Henry Ford's assembly line, cranking out cars. A Muslim American designed the skyscrapers of Chicago.

In 1957, when dedicating the Islamic center in Washington, D.C., President Eisenhower said, "I should like to assure you, my Islamic friends, that under the American Constitution ... and in American hearts...this place of worship, is just as welcome...as any other religion." (Applause.)

And perhaps the most pertinent fact, Muslim Americans enrich our lives today in every way. They're our neighbors, the teachers who inspire our children, the doctors who trust us with our health — future doctors like Sabah. They're scientists who win Nobel Prizes, young entrepreneurs who are creating new technologies that we use all the time. They're the sports heroes we cheer for -— like Muhammad Ali and Kareem Abdul-Jabbar, Hakeem Olajuwon. And by the way, when Team USA marches into the next Olympics, one of the Americans waving the red, white and blue — (applause) — will a fencing champion, wearing her hijab, Ibtihaj Muhammad, who is here today. Stand up. (Applause.)

I told her to bring home the gold. (Laughter.) Not to put any pressure on you. (Laughter.)

Muslim Americans keep us safe. They're our police and our firefighters. They're in homeland security, in our intelligence community. They serve honorably in our armed forces — meaning they fight and bleed and die for our freedom. Some rest in Arlington National Cemetery. (Applause.)

So Muslim Americans are some of the most resilient and patriotic Americans you'll ever meet. We're honored to have some of our proud Muslim American servicemembers here today. Please stand if you're here, so we can thank you for your service. (Applause.)

So part of the reason I want to lay out these facts is because, in the discussions that I was having with these incredibly accomplished young people, they were pointing that so often they felt invisible. And part of what we have to do is to lift up the contributions of the Muslim American community not when there's a problem, but all the time.

Our television shows should have some Muslim characters that are unrelated to national security — (applause) — because — it's not that hard to do. There was a time when there were no black people on television. And you can tell good stories while still representing the reality of our communities.

Now, we do have another fact that we have to acknowledge. Even as the overwhelming majority — and I repeat, the overwhelming majority — of the world's Muslims embrace Islam as a source of peace, it is undeniable that a small fraction of Muslims propagate a perverted interpretation of Islam. This is the truth.

Groups like al Qaeda and ISIL, they're not the first extremists in history to misuse God's name. We've seen it before, across faiths. But right now, there is a organized extremist element that draws selectively from Islamic texts, twists them in an attempt to justify their killing and their terror. They combine it with false claims that America and the West are at war with Islam. And this warped thinking that has found adherents around the world — including, as we saw, tragically, in Boston and Chattanooga and San Bernardino — is real. It's there. And it creates tensions and pressure that disproportionately burden the overwhelming majority of law-abiding Muslim citizens.

And the question then is, how do we move forward together? How do we keep our country strong and united? How do we defend ourselves against organizations that are bent on killing innocents? And it can't be the work of any one faith alone. It can't be just a burden on the Muslim community — although the Muslim community has to play a role. We all have responsibilities. So with the time I have left, I just want to suggest a few principles that I believe can guide us.

First, at a time when others are trying to divide us along lines of religion or sect, we have to reaffirm that most fundamental of truths: We are all God's children. We're all born equal, with inherent dignity.

And so often, we focus on our outward differences and we forget how much we share. Christians, Jews, Muslims — we're all, under our faiths, descendants of Abraham. So mere tolerance of different religions is not enough. Our faiths summon us to embrace our common humanity. "O mankind," the Koran teaches, we have "made you peoples and tribes that you may know one another." (Applause.) So all of us have the task of expressing our religious faith in a way that seeks to build bridges rather than to divide.

Second, as Americans, we have to stay true to our core values, and that includes freedom of religion for all faiths. I already mentioned our Founders, like Jefferson, knew that religious liberty is essential not only to protect religion but because religion helps strengthen our nation — if it is free, if it is not an extension of the state. Part of what's happened in the Middle East and North Africa and other places where we see sectarian violence is religion being a tool for another agenda — for power, for control. Freedom of religion helps prevent that, both ways — protects religious faiths, protects the state from — or those who want to take over the state from using religious animosity as a tool for their own ends.

That doesn't mean that those of us with religious faith should not be involved. We have to be active citizenry. But we have to respect the fact that we have freedom of religion.

Remember, many preachers and pastors fought to abolish the evil of slavery. People of faith advocated to improve conditions for workers and ban child labor. Dr. King was joined by people of many faiths, challenging us to live up to our ideals. And that civil activism, that civic participation that's the essence of our democracy, it is enhanced by freedom of religion.

Now, we have to acknowledge that there have been times where we have fallen short of our ideals. By the way, Thomas Jefferson's opponents tried to stir things up by suggesting he was a Muslim — so I was not the first — (applause.) No, it's true, it's true. Look it up. (Laughter.) I'm in good company. (Laughter.)

But it hasn't just been attacks of that sort that have been used. Mormon communities have been attacked throughout our history. Catholics, including, most prominently, JFK — John F. Kennedy — when he ran for President, was accused of being disloyal. There was a suggestion that he would be taking orders from the Pope as opposed to upholding his constitutional duties.

Anti-Semitism in this country has a sad and long history, and Jews were exclude routinely from colleges and professions and from public office.

And so if we're serious about freedom of religion — and I'm speaking now to my fellow Christians who remain the majority in this country

— we have to understand an attack on one faith is an attack on all our faiths. (Applause.) And when any religious group is targeted, we all have a responsibility to speak up. And we have to reject a politics that seeks to manipulate prejudice or bias, and targets people because of religion.

We've got to make sure that hate crimes are punished, and that the civil rights of all Americans are upheld. (Applause.) And just as faith leaders, including Muslims, must speak out when Christians are persecuted around the world — (applause) — or when anti-Semitism is on the rise — because the fact is, is that there are Christians who are targeted now in the Middle East, despite having been there for centuries, and there are Jews who've lived in places like France for centuries who now feel obliged to leave because they feel themselves under assault — sometimes by Muslims. We have to be consistent in condemning hateful rhetoric and violence against everyone. (Applause.) And that includes against Muslims here in the United States of America. (Applause.)

So none of us can be silent. We can't be bystanders to bigotry. And together, we've got to show that America truly protects all faiths.

Which brings me to my next point: As we protect our country from terrorism, we should not reinforce the ideas and the rhetoric of the terrorists themselves. I often hear it said that we need moral clarity in this fight. And the suggestion is somehow that if I would simply say, these are all Islamic terrorists, then we would actually have solved the problem by now, apparently. (Laughter.) Well, I agree, we actually do need moral clarity. Let's have some moral clarity. (Applause.)

Groups like ISIL are desperate for legitimacy. They try to portray themselves as religious leaders and holy warriors who speak for Islam. I refuse to give them legitimacy. We must never give them that legitimacy. (Applause.) They're not defending Islam. They're not defending

Muslims. The vast majority of the people they kill are innocent Muslim men, women and children. (Applause.)

And, by the way, the notion that America is at war with Islam ignores the fact that the world's religions are a part of who we are. We can't be at war with any other religion because the world's religions are a part of the very fabric of the United States, our national character. (Applause.)

So the best way for us to fight terrorism is to deny these organizations legitimacy and to show that here in the United States of America, we do not suppress Islam; we celebrate and lift up the success of Muslim Americans. That's how we show the lie that they're trying to propagate. (Applause.) We shouldn't play into terrorist propaganda. And we can't suggest that Islam itself is at the root of the problem. That betrays our values. It alienates Muslim Americans. It's hurtful to those kids who are trying to go to school and are members of the Boy Scouts, and are thinking about joining our military.

That kind of mindset helps our enemies. It helps our enemies recruit. It makes us all less safe. So let's be clear about that.

Now, finally, just as all Americans have a responsibility to reject discrimination — I've said this before — Muslims around the world have a responsibility to reject extremist ideologies that are trying to penetrate within Muslim communities.

Here at this mosque, and across our country and around the world, Muslim leaders are roundly and repeatedly and consistently condemning terrorism. And around the globe, Muslims who've dared to speak out have often been targeted and even killed. So those voices are there; we just have to amplify them more. (Applause.)

And it was interesting, in the discussion I had before I came out, some people said, why is there always a burden on us? When a young man in Charleston shoots African Americans in a church, there's not an expectation that every white person in America suddenly is explaining that they're not racist. They can Everybody is assumed to be horrified by that act. And I recognize that sometimes that doesn't feel fair.

But part of the answer is to make sure that the Muslim community in all of its variety, in all the good works that it's doing, in all the talent that's on display, that it's out there visible on a consistent basis — not just at a certain moment. (Applause.)

But what is also true is, is that there is a battle of hearts and minds that takes place — that is taking place right now, and American Muslims are better positioned than anybody to show that it is possible to be faithful to Islam and to be part of a pluralistic society, and to be on the cutting-edge of science, and to believe in democracy. (Applause.)

And so I would urge all of you not to see this as a burden, but as a great opportunity and a great privilege to show who you are. To use a little Christian expression — let your light shine. Because when you do you'll make clear that this is not a clash of civilizations between the West and Islam. This is a struggle between the peace-loving, overwhelming majority of Muslims around the world and a radical, tiny minority. And ultimately, I'm confident that the overwhelming majority will win that battle. (Applause.) Muslims will decide the future of your faith. And I'm confident in the direction that it will go.

But across the Islamic world, influential voices should consistently speak out with an affirmative vision of their faith. And it's happening. These are the voices of Muslim clerics who teach that Islam prohibits terrorism, for the Koran says whoever kills an innocent, it is as if he has killed all mankind. (Applause.) These are the voices of Muslim scholars, some of whom join us today, who know Islam has a tradition of respect for other faiths; and

Muslim teachers who point out that the first word revealed in the Koran — iqra — means "read" — to seek knowledge, to question assumptions. (Applause.)

Muslim political leaders have to push back on the lie that the West oppresses Muslims, and against conspiracy theories that says America is the cause of every ill in the Middle East. Now, that doesn't mean that Muslim Americans aren't free to criticize American — U.S. foreign policy. That's part of being an American. I promise you, as the President of the United States, I'm mindful that that is a healthy tradition that is alive and well in America. (Laughter.) But like leaders everywhere, these leaders have been offering, and need to continue to offer, a positive vision for progress, and that includes political and economic progress.

And we have to acknowledge that much of the violence in places like the Middle East is now turning into fights between sects — Shia, Sunni and others — where differences are often exploited to serve political agendas, as I said earlier. And this bloodshed is destroying Muslim families and communities, and there has to be global pressure to have the vision and the courage to end this kind of thinking and this approach to organizing political power.

It's not historically unique. It's happened in every part of the world — from Northern Ireland to Africa, to Asia, to right here in the United States — in the past. But it is something that we have to fight against.

And we know it's possible. Across the history of Islam, different sects traditionally have lived and thrived together peacefully. And in many parts of the world they do today, including here in the United States.

Like people of all religions, Muslims living their faith in a modern, pluralistic world are called upon to uphold human rights, to make sure that everyone has opportunity. That includes the aspirations of women and youth and all people. If we expect our own dignity to be respected, so must we respect the dignity of others. (Applause.)

So let me conclude by saying that as Muslim communities stand up for the future that you believe in, that you exhibit in your daily lives, as you teach your children, America will be your partner. We will — I will

— do everything I can to lift up the multiplicity of Muslim voices that promote pluralism and peace. (Applause.) We will continue to reach out to young Muslims around the world, empowering them with science and technology and entrepreneurship, so they can pursue their God-given potential, and help build up their communities and provide opportunity. It's why we will continue to partner with Muslim American communities — not just to help you protect against extremist threats, but to expand health care and education and opportunity — (applause) — because that's the best way to build strong, resilient communities.

Our values must guide us in this work. Engagement with Muslim American communities must never be a cover for surveillance. (Applause.) We can't give in to profiling entire groups of people. There's no one single profile of terrorists. We can't securitize our entire relationship with Muslim Americans. We can't deal with you solely through the prism of law enforcement. We've got to build trust and mutual respect. That's how we'll keep our communities strong and our communities united.

As I was in discussion with the young people before I came in here, I said this will be a process. Law enforcement has a tough job. Some of these groups are specifically trying to target Muslim youth. We're going to have to be partners in this process. There will be times where the relationship is clumsy or mishandled. But I want you to know that from the President to the FBI Director, to everybody in law enforcement, my directive and their understanding is, is that this is something we have to do together. And if we don't do it well, then we're actually not making ourselves safer; we're making ourselves less safe.

And here, I want to speak directly to the young people who may be listening. In our lives, we all have many identities. We are sons and daughters, and brothers and sisters. We're classmates; Cub Scout troop members. We're followers of our faith. We're citizens of our country.

And today, there are voices in this world, particularly over the Internet, who are constantly claiming that you have to choose between your identities — as a Muslim, for example, or an American. Do not believe them. If you're ever wondering whether you fit in here, let me say it as clearly as I can, as President of the United States: You fit in here — right here. (Applause.) You're right where you belong. You're part of America, too. (Applause.) You're not Muslim or American. You're Muslim and American. (Applause.)

Don't grow cynical. Don't respond to ignorance by embracing a world view that suggests you must choose between your faith and your patriotism. Don't believe that you have to choose between your best impulses and somehow embrace a world view that pits us against each other — or, even worse, glorifies violence. Understand your power to bring about change. Stay engaged in your community. Help move our country forward — your country forward. (Applause.)

We are blessed to live in a nation where even if we sometimes stumble, even if we sometimes fall short, we never stop striving for our ideals. We keep moving closer to that more perfect union. We're a country where, if you work hard and if you play by the rules, you can ultimately make it, no matter who you are or how you pray. It may not always start off even in the race, but here, more than any place else, there's the opportunity to run that race.

And as we go forward, I want every Muslim American to remember you are not alone. Your fellow Americans stand with you — just as Sabah described her friends after she decided that she was going to start wearing a hijab. That's not unusual. Because just as so often we only hear about Muslims after a terrorist attack, so often we only hear about Americans' response to Muslims after a hate crime has happened, we don't always hear about the extraordinary respect and love and community that so many Americans feel.

I'm thinking about the seven-year-old boy in Texas who emptied his piggy bank to help a mosque that had been vandalized. (Applause.) Or all the faith communities that rallied around Muslim Americans after the tragedy in Chapel Hill. The churches and the synagogues standing shoulder-to-shoulder with their local mosques, including the woman carrying a sign saying "We love our Muslim neighbors." Think of our men and women in uniform who, when they heard that a little girl was afraid because she's a Muslim, sent her a message — "I Will Protect You." (Applause.)

I want every American to remember how Muslim communities are standing up for others, as well. Because right now, as we speak, there are Muslims in Kenya who saved Christians from terrorists, and Muslims who just met in Morocco to protect religious minorities, including Christians and Jews. (Applause.) The good people of this mosque helped this city move forward after the turmoil of last year. Muslim Americans across the country helped African American churches rebuild after arson.

Remember the Muslim Americans in Boston who reached out to victims of the Marathon bombing; the Muslim Americans across the country who raised money for the families of San Bernardino; the Muslim Americans in Chattanooga who honored our fallen servicemembers, one of them saying, "in the name of God, the God of Abraham, Moses, Jesus, and Muhammad, God bless our fallen heroes." (Applause.)

We are one American family. We will rise and fall together. It won't always be easy. There will be times where our worst impulses are given voice. But I believe that ultimately, our best voices will win out. And that gives me confidence and faith in the future. (Applause.)

After more than 200 years, our blended heritage, the patchwork quilt which is America, that is not a weakness, that is one of our greatest strengths. It's what makes us a beacon to the world. It's what led that mother who wrote to me — the one who worries about her young daughter — it led her to end her letter with hope, despite her fears. She said, "I still believe in one nation, under God, indivisible, with liberty and justice for all." (Applause.)

May God's peace be upon you. May God bless the United States of America. Thank you very much, everybody. (Applause.)

END

1:52 P.M. EST

Obama's Final Ramadan Statement

The White House

Office of the Press Secretary

For Immediate Release

June 05, 2016

Statement by the President on the Occasion of Ramadan

As another new moon heralds the start of the holy month of Ramadan, Michelle and I extend our best wishes to Muslims across the United States and around the world.

For many, this month is an opportunity to focus on reflection and spiritual growth, forgiveness, patience and resilience, compassion for those less fortunate, and unity across communities. Each lesson is profound on its own, and taken together forms a harmonious whole. It's also a time of year that brings some of the best dishes to the table across the world as families and neighbors gather for *iftar*.

Here in the United States, we are blessed with Muslim communities as diverse as our nation itself. There are those whose heritage can be traced back to the very beginning of our nation, as well as those who have only just arrived. Doctors, lawyers, artists, teachers, scientists, community organizers, public servants, and military members, each night will all break their fasts together in cities across America.

As Muslim Americans celebrate the holy month, I am reminded that we are one American family. I stand firmly with Muslim American communities in rejection of the voices that seek to divide us or limit our religious freedoms or civil rights. I stand committed to safeguarding the civil rights of all Americans no matter their religion or appearance. I stand in celebration of our common humanity and dedication to peace and justice for all.

And in this month of reflection, we cannot forget the millions of lives that have been displaced by conflict and struggle, across the world and in our own backyards. Far too many Muslims may not be able to observe Ramadan from the comfort of their own homes this year or afford to celebrate Eid with their children. We must continue working together to alleviate the suffering of these individuals. This sacred time reminds us of our common obligations to uphold the dignity of every human being. We will continue to welcome immigrants and refugees into our nation, including those who are Muslim.

As I have done throughout my presidency, I look forward to opening the doors of the White House to Muslim Americans during this special occasion – this year for an Eid celebration marking the end of Ramadan. I can think of no better way to mark my Administration's last celebration of Ramadan as President than to honor the contributions of Muslims in America and across the world for Eid. Ramadan Kareem.

America's Leading LGBT Activist

Obama Administration Record for the LGBT Community [2]

https://www.whitehouse.gov/sites/default/files/docs/lgbt_record.pdf

"Every single American — gay, straight, lesbian, bisexual, transgender — every single American deserves to be treated equally in the eyes of the law and in the eyes of our society. It's a pretty simple proposition."

-President Barack Obama, October 1, 2011

Obama site touts 40 accomplishments for gays— 2009 to 2012 [3]

http://www.bpnews.net/37679/
obama-site-touts-40-accomplishments-for-gays.

Obama's proclamation for Lesbian, Gay, Bisexual, And Transgender (LGBT) Pride Month, 2016 [4]

For Immediate Release

May 31, 2016

Presidential Proclamation LGBT Pride Month, 2016

Source: **White House**

LESBIAN, GAY, BISEXUAL, AND TRANSGENDER PRIDE MONTH, 2016

- - - - - - -

BY THE PRESIDENT OF THE UNITED STATES OF AMERICA

A PROCLAMATION

Since our founding, America has advanced on an unending path toward becoming a more perfect Union. This journey, led by forward-thinking individuals who have set their sights on reaching for a brighter tomorrow, has never been easy or smooth.

The fight for dignity and equality for lesbian, gay, bisexual, and transgender (LGBT) people is reflected in the tireless dedication of advocates and allies who strive to forge a more inclusive society.

They have spurred **sweeping progress by changing hearts and minds and by demanding equal treatmen**t — under our laws, from our courts, and in our politics.

This month, we recognize all they have done to bring us to this point, and we recommit to bending the arc of our Nation toward justice.

Last year's landmark Supreme Court decision guaranteeing marriage equality in all 50 States was a historic victory for LGBT Americans, ensuring dignity for same-sex couples and greater equality across State lines.

For every partnership that was not previously recognized under the law and for every American who was denied their basic civil rights, this monumental ruling instilled newfound hope, affirming the belief that **we are all more free when we are treated as equals.**

LGBT individuals deserve to know their country stands beside them. That is why my Administration is striving to <u>better understand the needs of LGBT adults and to provide affordable, welcoming, and supportive housing to aging LGBT Americans.</u>

It is also why we oppose subjecting minors to the harmful practice of conversion therapy, and why we are continuing **to promote equality and foster safe and supportive learning environments for all students.**

We remain committed to addressing health disparities in the LGBT community — gay and bisexual men and transgender women of color are at a particularly high risk for HIV, and we have worked to strengthen our National HIV/AIDS Strategy to reduce new infections, increase access to care, and improve health outcomes for people living with HIV.

Despite the extraordinary progress of the past few years, **LGBT Americans still face discrimination simply for being who they are.**

I signed an Executive Order in 2014 that prohibits discrimination against Federal employees and contractors on the basis of sexual orientation or gender identity.

I urge the Congress to enact legislation that builds upon the progress we have made, **because no one should live in fear of losing their job simply because of who they are or who they love.**

And our commitment to combatting discrimination against the LGBT community does not stop at our borders: Advancing the fair treatment of all people has long been a cornerstone of American diplomacy, and **we have made defending and promoting the human rights of LGBT individuals a priority in our engagement across the globe.**

In line with **America's commitment to the notion that all people should be treated fairly and with respect, champions of this cause at home and abroad are upholding the simple truth that LGBT rights are human rights.**

There remains much work to do to extend the promise of our country to every American, but because of the acts of courage of the millions who came out and spoke out to demand justice and of those who quietly toiled and pushed for progress, our Nation has made great strides in recognizing what these brave individuals long knew to be true in their hearts — **that love is love and that no person should be judged by anything but the content of their character.**

During Lesbian, Gay, Bisexual, and Transgender Pride Month, as Americans wave their flags of pride high and march boldly forward in parades and demonstrations, **let us celebrate how far we have come and reaffirm our steadfast belief in the equal dignity of all Americans.**

NOW, THEREFORE, I, BARACK OBAMA, President of the United States of America, by virtue of the authority vested in me by the Constitution and the laws of the United States, do hereby proclaim June 2016 as Lesbian, Gay, Bisexual, and Transgender Pride Month. **I call upon the people of the United States to eliminate prejudice everywhere it exists, and to celebrate the great diversity of the American people.**

IN WITNESS WHEREOF, I have hereunto set my hand this thirty-first day of May, in the year of our Lord two thousand sixteen, and of the Independence of the United States of America the two hundred and fortieth.

BARACK OBAMA

America's Most Biblically-Hostile U. S. President— Wall Builders

To review the following examples visit the following website:

http://www.wallbuilders.com/libissuesarticles.asp?id=106938

1. **Acts of hostility toward people of biblical faith**

2. **Acts of hostility from the Obama-led military toward people of biblical faith**

3. **Acts of hostility toward biblical values**

4. **Acts of preferentialism for Islam**

Many of these actions are literally unprecedented—this is the first time they have happened in four centuries of American history. The hostility of President Obama toward biblical faith and values is without equal from any previous American president.

Endnotes

1. *Muslim Apologist:*

   http://usherald.com/
   11-jaw-dropping-obama-quotes-on-america-and-islam/

2. *Obama Administration Record for the LGBT Community*

   https://www.whitehouse.gov/sites/default/files/docs/lgbt_record.
   pdf

3. *Obama site touts 40 accomplishments for gays – Baptist Press*
   http://www.bpnews.net/37679/
   obama-site-touts-40-accomplishments-for-gays

4. *Obama's proclamation for Lesbian, Gay, Bisexual, And Transgender (LGBT) Pride Month, 2016*

   https://www.whitehouse.gov/the-press-office/2016/05/31/
   presidential-proclamation-lgbt-pride-month-2016

ABOUT THE AUTHOR

William Koenig has been a White House correspondent for 15 and a half years.

His Internet news service World Watch Daily (http://watch.org), which was established in 1996, has readers and e-mail subscribers in all 50 states and 105 countries.

He writes a weekly 15-page news report called "Koenig's Eye View from the White House," that focuses on world news that is biblically relevant and White House news from a Christian perspective.

He authored *Eye to Eye — Facing the Consequences of Dividing Israel,* which is in its 24th printing.

William and his wife Claudia are frequent travelers to Israel. They have traveled to 32 states and ten countries speaking on the biblical significance of Israel and the times that we live in.

He graduated from Arizona State University with a B.S. in Communications.

He and Claudia live in the Washington, D.C. area.

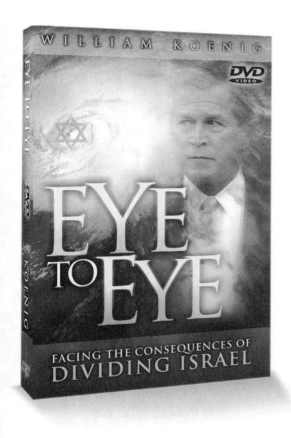